Esther, Portraits of the Old and New Covenants

Jim Dent

Published by Jim Dent, 2023.

While every precaution has been taken in the preparation of this book, the publisher assumes no responsibility for errors or omissions, or for damages resulting from the use of the information contained herein.

ESTHER, PORTRAITS OF THE OLD AND NEW COVENANTS

First edition. December 1, 2023.

Copyright © 2023 Jim Dent.

Written by Jim Dent.

I dedicate this book to my wife Ali.

Esther, Literary Reflections on the Bible

By Jim Dent
Copyright 2023

Introduction

The book of Esther is fascinating and encouraging for a host of reasons, and it has become one of my favorite books in the Bible. It has layers upon layers of Biblical themes that portray God's covenantal relationship with his chosen people. In it we see pictures of the old and new covenants, and accordingly it is a microcosm of God's redemptive story that we see God portray through the whole Bible, beginning with a husband and wife behaving badly and ending with the salvation of God's people and a picture of a glorified Church. In between, we have scenes in which the characters reveal types of God, Christ, the Antichrist, husbands, wives, and the Church. Among the heroes and villains, we see a portrait of a woman as one of the greatest heroines in history. Every time I study this book, I gain new insights that evoke both tears and joyous laughter.

Literary Elements

I will explore the literary story elements of this book, not all the elements, but the ones that strike me as the key elements that make this such a gripping, enduring story. God is the master storyteller. He uses stories great and small to teach us about who he is and who we are. He does this because stories stick with us, piercing us to our inmost being, appealing to both our mind and emotions. Being created in his image, we love stories, and we like to hear them and tell them. Our lives, in fact, are great, elaborate stories made up of tens of thousands of scenes. We are writing them every day with the words we use and the decisions we make.

God teaches us and relates to us through story, and he uses all the means at his disposal to make stories engage us and delight us more completely. For instance, foreshadowing in a story increases suspense, mystery, and connectivity. A story can be fine without it but is much richer when it is there. The beauty is that literary elements tell us something about the nature and character of God and his love for us.

One of the literary concepts that I will explore and revisit throughout this study is the story structure of The Hero's Journey. Whether it is Biblical characters, mythical characters, book characters, movie characters or you and me, all heroes have a journey that has distinct, observable stages that, more or less, follow a consistent order. It is a phenomenon that was created by God. I like to compare this concept to the 5 Stages of Grief that were first defined by researcher Elizabeth Kubler-Ross. Both are life-journey processes that follow an ordained order, and when we understand them, they can be a tremendous benefit to us.

Joseph Campbell first described The Hero's Journey in his book called, <u>The Hero with a Thousand Faces</u>, 1949. Campbell asserts that heroes in the Bible, myth and the rest of history go through 17 stages in their journey to becoming heroes. Sometimes heroes skip one or more stages, or they bog down in a stage. Often times heroes go back and repeat some stages. The order of the stages may vary. It is not a one-size-fits-all construct that always follows a strict order. Rather it is a framework that helps us understand what goes into the making of a hero, sort of like the ingredients that go into the making of a cake.

Campbell also borrowed the concept of character archetypes from Carl Jung, and he expanded on how there are particular character archetypes that fulfill very specific roles in The Hero's Journey. We will expand on this more later, but one example is the character archetype of the mentor. Heroes almost always have a mentor. Think about Obi Wan Kenobi from Star Wars and Gandalf from Lord of the Rings. Mentors play the role of coaching a hero, and they often help a hero when they get stuck in a particular stage of the journey.

After Campbell's ground-breaking book, many other writers wrote their own versions about the hero's journey. One of my favorites is a book by Christopher Vogler called, *The Writer's Journey,* 1998. Vogler condenses Campbell's seventeen stages to twelve stages. His book highlights how writers can recognize and use the construct of The Hero's Journey to write more compelling stories that fit the flow of normal events in life. Vogler has contributed to over 10,000 screen plays and has worked on blockbuster stories such as The Lion King and Beauty and the Beast. He has influenced many more, such as Star Wars.

You might ask, "What does this have to do with the Bible and Esther?" There are several answers. First, as a storyteller, God uses every means at hand to tell more compelling, memorable stories to increase the impact on our lives. Understanding this helps us appreciate and enjoy Him more. Second, God calls all of us to be heroes, and as we understand the Hero's Journey elements, we can expect and react to the pitfalls that await us, and we can anticipate the character archetypes that may help or hinder us along the way. How often do you ask yourself, "Why is this happening? What is going on? Why am I encountering resistance instead of support?" Such times simply may be elements of your own hero's journey.

Let's take a quick look at the stages of The Hero's Journey. The twelve stages of the hero's journey, according to Christopher Vogler, are as follows. (<u>The Writer's Journey</u>, Vogler, C., 1998, 2nd Edition, page 14)

1. The Ordinary World.
2. Call to adventure.
3. Refusal of the Call.
4. Meeting with the mentor.
5. Crossing the first threshold.
6. Tests, allies, and enemies.
7. Approach to the inmost cave
8. Ordeal.
9. Reward.

10. The road back.
11. Resurrection.
12. Return with the elixir.

The Character Archetypes are as follows.

1. Hero
2. Herald
3. Mentor
4. Ally
5. Shapeshifter
6. Shadow
7. Trickster
8. Threshold guardian

We will unpack these further as we encounter them in Esther's story. Esther was one of the best heroines in history, a heroine that never took up a sword or weapon. Maybe she was not the perfect Hebrew maiden, but she grew into a heroine. This growth is what we refer to the character arch in literary study. She models for us a journey that should inspire people from all walks of life, especially women.

Christ is the best hero that humankind has ever known. He is the perfect hero, one who never wavered, never balked at his call, and never failed. If we study his life, we can trace the stages of the Hero's Journey. In the final stage of his journey, he returned with the elixir. Christ brought salvation to a dying world.

All of us have the call to be like Christ, and part of that call is to bring the very same elixir to a suffering world, the blood of Christ. Our call is to bring the comfort and call of the Gospel to our family, friends, town, country and farthest most parts of the world. My hope is that by studying Esther's journey, we can find inspiration and insight to complete our journeys and get that wonderful acknowledgement from God as stated in Matthew 25:23: "His master said to him, "Well done, good and faithful servant. You have been faithful over a little; I will set you over much. Enter into the joy of your master.""

Historical Context

Modern scholars place the events of Esther between 483 and 473 B. C. The book opens with accounts of events in the life of King Ahasuerus. Some historians believe Ahasuerus is Xerxes I, King of Persia. Others believe he is the son of Xerxes, Artaxerxes. Although it is not critical to our discussion, I tend to believe Ahasuerus is the historical King Xerxes, who reigned over the Persian empire from 486 to 465 B.C. The text tells us that at the time of this story, the empire had 27 Provinces from India to Ethiopia, quite a large area.

The timeline of Esther takes place in the gap between the sixth and seventh chapters of the book of Ezra. It is the time of Persian occupation of Israel and Judah. Under King Darius, the father of Xerxes, Israelites rebuilt the temple in Jerusalem. Darius issued a decree that allowed some of the Hebrews to return to the City of David to rebuild the temple, and the son of Xerxes, Artaxerxes, issued a decree that allowed for a second return-migration of Hebrews to their homeland. It is between these two decrees that the compelling events happened in the book of Esther, which include the saving of God's people.

Xerxes ruled during the territorial apex of the Persian Empire. He ruled over Egypt and even temporarily overran mainland Greece, but he was defeated in his conquest to rule Greece. The king vacillated between being a decent man, to sometimes being very ruthless in his treatment of others, at one time beheading the architects of a bridge that was destroyed by a storm. Xerxes seemed to lack any clear convictions about anything, acting on a whim or at the advice of his royal advisors. At times the advice he listened to was not sound or in his best interest. Xerxes died by assassination at the hands of Artabanus, the commander of his royal bodyguard.

Observations

The book of Esther is unique in all the Bible because it does not mention Yahweh or any other deity. Many theologians have had negative views on the book and its rightful place in the canon of scripture. Even Martin Luther did not care for the book. He said in his Table Talks, "I am so hostile to this book that I wish it did not exist, for it Judaizes too much and has too much heathen naughtiness." His general belief was that it lacked the saving truths of scripture.

Esther was indeed included in the cannon of Christian scripture. It was even part of the Hebrew canon and Hebrews regarded it above the books of prophecy. This disparity of regard for the book seems to be related to the Hebrew versus gentile conflict. Some see it as putting too much emphasis on Hebrew salvation from the hands of the gentiles. I regard this as myopic, a failure to see that the story shows how God deals with his chosen people, all of them, Israel, and the New Israel.

Esther also offers us another dimension of authenticity in the ways that it depicts Persian culture. We read repeatedly about the role of eunuchs in the royal palace. They often are the ones that attend to the personal needs of the king and queen. Kings frequently retained eunuchs in their royal courts due to their lack of testosterone, which reduced the risk of violent or aggressive behavior towards the king, making them less threatening. Kings liked to have eunuchs attend to their queens because there would not be a temptation for an unfaithful wife to seek sexual gratification from them. Ultimately, both these benefits served the king.

The text demonstrates the Persians had opulent, lavish parties in which they used gold goblets and utensils. These often all were unique works of craftsmanship. During such parties, as well as during any dining occasion in the palace, the Persians drank wine to excess. Special note is made in Esther 1:8 that, in this particular party thrown by Ahasuerus, there was no compulsion to drink according to custom, meaning that the king did not compel anyone to abstain from alcohol or consume it to excess.

The Persian customs that we see depicted in Esther portray a culture that is worldly, fleshly, and carnal. This stands in contrast to the Hebrew custom of living a wholesome life, devoted to God. We see this clearly illustrated in the book of Daniel, when Daniel served in the courts of the Babylonians and subsequently the Persians. It is a contrast between a worldly culture and a godly culture. Esther brings those cultures colliding together with fascinating results. It is a fine illustration of the teaching that Paul gives us in Romans chapter 8. For many Christians, when we face the conflict of how to live, the flesh often wins the day. Although the young maiden Esther conforms to the culture around her, living more of a worldly lifestyle, she becomes a heroine of epic stature. She grows into a heroine that seems to live according to the Spirit, not the flesh. In this sense, she is a lot like David, a hero with feet of clay.

Esther and The Gospel

The book of Esther depicts characters that are more significant in their type than in their temporal identity. King Xerxes, Haman, Mordecai, and Esther are all chess pieces on God's grand chessboard of history. They are real people, but they portray character types of God, Christ, the Church, the Antichrist, Adam, Eve, and husband, and wife. These very real people represent figures far greater than themselves and offer us a glimpse into God's kingdom. (His People, in His place, under His rule).

Since Esther is such a short story with a limited number of characters, each of the characters reflect multiple other characters in the Bible. Think about the analogy of a football team that only has 11 players. Each person must be called on to play a role on offence, another role on defense, and other roles on special teams. The characters in Esther portray multiple characters in God's redemptive story. They give us pictures of The Gospel. For instance, the character of Esther represents a type of bride, a type of the Church or at times a type of Christ. Some of the other characters portray multiple types as well, depending on the scene. We see the characters in Esther's story point us to elements of The Gospel and God's redemptive plan for his people.

1

Esther 1:1-9

Context

To better understand the spiritual, and cultural context of the book of Esther, let's look at the historical and Biblical events that took place in the years leading up to our story. We will start with a brief review of the past 130 years.

In 612 BC, the Babylonians overthrew the Assyrians, who ruled much of the middle east, ushering in the Babylonian Empire. In 605 BC, the Babylonians overthrew the Assyrians in Egypt. It was during this time of Babylonian conquest that Israel and Judah fell into exile, and the Babylonians took many of the most promising Hebrew leaders and youths into captivity. We can read about this in the book of Daniel. Daniel was one of the promising youths taken into captivity by the Babylonian King, Nebuchadnezzar, who made Daniel one of his chief advisors after he interpreted a dream for him. Daniel served in the king's court until the overthrow of King Belshazzar after the handwriting on the wall incident in 539 BC, when the Medes and the Persians defeated the Babylonians. The Hebrew people remained in exile and under Persian rule after the Persians conquered the Babylonians.

Fast forward to the book of Ezra. In 538 BC, the Persian King Cyrus declared that those people of Israel and Judah who wanted to return to their homeland may do so, and he gave them permission to rebuild the temple. Although Cyrus wanted to let the Hebrews rebuild the temple, his opponents thwarted their efforts. In the year 522 BC, Darius assumed the rule of Persia from Cyrus, and in his sixth year of rule, he made a decree to rebuild the temple, and he allocated the funds necessary to do so. They rebuilt the temple in 515 BC, and he ordered that all the gold and silver bowls, goblets and ceremonial fixtures of the temple that were taken by the Babylonians to be returned to the temple. At the temple dedication ceremony, Darius provided 100 bulls, 200 rams, and 400 lambs as burnt offerings. This brings us the end of chapter 6 of Ezra.

The events of the book of Esther take place between chapters 6 and 7 of Ezra, covering the period from 483 BC to 473 BC. Chapter 7 of Ezra picks up when Artaxerxes, the son of Xerxes I, gives a decree for a second wave of Hebrews to return to their homeland.

Four other books of the Bible, in addition to Esther, cover portions of this period of history. Ezra, Nehemiah, Haggai, and Zechariah all fit in between Daniel and the prophetic book of Malachi (432-425 BC). After Malachi, we have over 400 years of Biblical silence before the events of the New Testament begin. It was a flurry of prophetic activity, of God calling His people to repent before he sends His son.

The book of Esther begins, in about 483 BC, with the account of a huge celebration thrown by King Ahasuerus. In verse 1, we learn he ruled over 127 provinces from India to Ethiopia. This is seven more provinces than existed when Cyrus was king and appointed Daniel to rule over a third of the 120 Persian provinces. It is a large kingdom, which is at the zenith of Persian geographical rule.

Observations

The king's palace was in the capital city of Susa, and it was in Ahasueras' 3rd year of reign that he held a party for 180 days to celebrate the "riches of his royal glory," for which he invited all the nobles and governors of his kingdom. We can conclude a few things about this celebration. First, Ahasuerus was quite vain to allot half a year to celebrate his glory. As all humankind was created in the image of God, it implies that we are designed to seek glory. The pure, obedient, and holy expression of this is to seek God's glory in our words and actions. Conversely, the sinful and rebellious manifestation of this inclination is to seek our own glory, which amounts to idolatry and rebellion against the one who truly deserves glory. The king, in all of his pomp and pride, sought his own glory, robbing God of the glory that is due to him. Right away the writer sets the scene of a king in the grip of sin and throwing a lengthy, lascivious party.

We can conclude that the Persian Empire had abundant wealth. They gave the celebration for a large multitude. The armies of Persia and Media were invited, as well as the nobles and governors. It could not have been cheap to entertain such a large number for half of a year. No doubt the king had to quarter this great multitude. Again, we have a picture of an extremely indulgent, flesh-pleasing, worldly affair.

The 180-day celebration came to a climax, a 7-day feast in the court of the king's palace. The text in verse five says the feast was for all, great and small. They excluded no one. Verse six describes the beautiful decorations in the king's palace, telling of white curtains, violet wall hangings and purple curtains on rods of silver. There are marble pillars, couches of gold, mosaic pavement and all kinds of precious stones. It was a luxurious decorator's showcase, all dripping with the vestiges that come with great wealth. The king treated the party goers to his wine, which was of special quality, not the normal, every-day wine of the palace. They drank wine from gold goblets that were all different, indicating that each one was the product of an artist-craftsman.

At royal parties, excessive wine consumption was the norm. However, on this occasion, a new edict allowed guests to drink without any pressure. This edict offered the freedom for individuals to choose to moderate or refrain from drinking altogether, perhaps to sustain themselves for the entire six-month party. With no compulsory rules regarding alcohol, it's likely that they did not enforce moderation. As a result, it is clear that many would take the liberty to indulge excessively.

Verse nine tells us that Queen Vashti also gave a feast for women in the palace that belonged to King Ahasuerus. This is our first indication that all is not well with the royal marriage. The text is clear that the palace belonged to the king and that his queen did not share in ownership of the kingdom. And for whatever reason, she did not feel like she could, or would want to, entertain her women friends at the king's feast, so she had her own feast and party. To some extent, we might conclude that Queen Vashti was persona non grata in the palace.

Literary Elements
Theme

Several literary elements emerge in these first nine verses. First, scene one establishes a theme of feasts. The writer uses the word feast three times in the first nine verses. This reminds the reader of bounty of food that Adam and Eve had in the Garden of Eden.

Mood

Second, the author sets the mood of the first scene with the description of luxury and wealth, as described above. The description of the palace in all its beauty and completeness reminds us of the beauty and completeness, the self-sufficiency of the Garden of Eden. We can sum it up by saying it is a mood of abundance.

Setting

Third, the author portrays the setting in the capital city of Susa. These three elements paint a picture of a type of city that could be a type of the city we shall see in the new heavens and the new earth, the New Jerusalem, described in chapter 21 of Revelation.

Esther and The Gospel

At the time of The Fall, after Adam and Eve ate of the forbidden fruit, God put a curse on all of humankind, that man would rule over his wife and that his wife's desire would be for her husband. This means that her desire would be to rule over him, leading to the ever-present conflict for power and control between husbands and wives. The segregated feasts for the king and queen could indicate there was conflict and competition between the spouses. It also emphasizes the mine and yours mentality; they did not share their possessions. This not only represents the conflict in their marriage, but it also portrays the conflict with God's kingdom. God says that husbands and wives are joint heirs of God's grace (I Peter 3:7). God's grace encompasses all his benefits, including being heirs to his kingdom. Clearly, Vashti was not an equal heir to Ahasuerus' kingdom.

Verse nine causes us to reflect on Adam and Eve and the conflict that married couples face. Moreover, King Ahasuerus represents a type of a bad husband, like Adam was. He did not protect or care for his bride the way God intended for him. Later in the story of Esther, we can contrast this behavior with Ahasuerus' actions that portray him as a type of a good husband. The Holy Spirit, as author of this book, sets up a high-level view of how God deals with his people from Adam to Christ, who redeems his bride, the Church. The story sets up a picture of how the king does not act as a good husband. In a sense, he is like the first Adam. Later in this story of Esther, we see how a good husband treats his wife, which is a picture of the Second Adam. This becomes a secondary theme in the Esther story.

2
Esther 1:10-22

Context

The celebration has gone on for six months in Susa, and Ahasuerus brings it to an end on the seventh day with a climactic feast. Queen Vashti was still having her separate party with her lady friends. Ahasuerus, who was merry from drinking wine, ordered his seven attending eunuchs to summon Queen Vashti to appear before him to show off her beauty. She refused to come, leading to the king becoming angry.

Observations

Vashti apparently refused to join him and his inebriated friends, parading herself before them merely as eye candy. There are so many things wrong with the king's request that it is hard to know where to start. My first question is, why did it take so long for the king to invite the queen to be a part of his celebration? Seven days, really?

One can only imagine what kinds of relational problems existed for the king and queen that he would not invite her to be by his side until the seventh day of a feast. Is the only reason he chose her to be his queen because she was beautiful to look at? Did she not have any other redeeming qualities? It is possible that he did not value any other of her attributes of her character than her good looks. Men can be that way. It could also be possible that she did not have any other redeeming qualities than her appearance. The text does not address this issue. Maybe this king did not value women at all, other than objects to be possessed. Another viewpoint might be that what may have started out as a good marriage descended into one in which neither husband nor wife displayed the character of a godly husband and wife. After all, without God, none of us can have a marriage as God intended it.

The king "commanded" his eunuchs to bring Queen Vashti before him in her royal crown to show the princes and people her beauty. Some commentators think that this command was for Vashti to wear her royal crown and only her royal crown. If indeed he summoned her to appear before the court naked, this would have been a terrible insult to his wife and queen. Yet, either way, asking her to parade before the king's court, even with clothes on, completely objectified her. Imagine how she must have felt? She was having her own feast with her lady-friends, when on the final day of the feast, King Ahasuerus asked her to walk the catwalk for him and a bunch of drunken men. She must have felt hurt and furious.

Unfortunately, she responded with indignation and refused to come. This enraged the king and "his anger burned within him." (v 12) The king was clearly wrong in the way he treated his queen, and she arguably could have found a better response that would not have resulted in banishment. After all, he was the sovereign ruler of the land, holding the power to deal out reward or death. Queen Vashti could have tried to speak to her king and explain to him how dishonoring the queen dishonors the kingdom. Or even show up and make an appearance and take it up with him when he was sober. Yet, her pride ruled the day and she bore the very painful consequences.

The king, in his anger, did not respond like a leader. Rather than diffusing the situation, he made it worse by asking for counsel from his "wise men." He gave over his right to make a kingly decision to whomever made the strongest argument for a vengeful response. He asked them what he should do with his wife. I have heard many men give another man advice on what to do about his wife, but the problem is that the one giving the advice does not have to live with her afterwards. Such advice is almost always bad, unless it comes from a very godly man. But that was not the case in this situation. The advice came from a drunk man who was disappointed in not having the burlesque show that he thought he was going to get.

Memucan prevailed in his argument about what Ahasuerus should do with Vashti. He contended that her insolence and disobedience to the king would spread to all women of the kingdom, leading to all wives everywhere in rebelling against their spouses. Such advice could only come from a man who completely failed to engender love and loyalty from his own wife. No wonder this is what he suggested.

Memucan proposed that the offense was not only against the king, but against all men in the kingdom. He said it would cause all women to look at their husbands with contempt. The real truth is that all the women who have husbands that treat their wives like Ahasuerus, already look at their husbands with contempt. Conversely, if they had godly husbands, nothing could change the way they look at them! The profound message here for all marriages is we should try to outdo one another is showing deference and honor.

The king's counselors convinced him to make a decree that Queen Vashti would never come before him again, and that the king would find another woman more fitting for the role of queen. One of the immutable characteristics of a decree by a Persian king is that it could never be reversed, changed, or ignored, even by the king who gave it. Some commentators believe that the decree that Queen Vashti would never come before the king again was a euphemism for a death sentence. It was a nice way to say that he had her beheaded. He made the decree and later, when he was sober, his heart ached over not having her anymore. His decree was final.

Hence, the king made the decree, and he wrote the decree in every language represented in his kingdom and sent it out to all 127 provinces, according to the language of those living in them. His zeal must have pleased Memucan and the other men of the king's court, for now they had a decree that dictated that their wives must submit to their husbands, which is an abomination in light of the whole counsel of scripture that adjures husbands and wives to submit to one another in deference and meekness.

Literary Elements
Theme

The number seven represents completeness in the Bible. We see a theme is the second part of the first chapter that centers on the number seven. On the seventh day of the feast, Ahasuerus sent seven eunuchs to Queen Vashti and subsequently consulted with seven princes of the kingdom. suggesting that the feast was complete, the entourage of messengers sent to the queen was complete and the number of counselors to the king was complete. Perhaps the mentioning of all these sevens might cause a reader to reflect on the seven days of creation.

Mood

The mood we see in the second part of chapter one is compelling. In the opening verses, we see a mood of lavish abundance, a mood of gracious provision. The Descriptions of the complete beauty and lavishness of the palace reminds us of the complete perfection of the garden before the fall. The mood in the second half of the chapter is one of legalism. It reminds us of the legal implications that came to Adam and Eve after the fall. Ahasuerus makes a decree or law that cannot change, and the law results in banishment and death, just as God banished Adam and Eve from the garden the king banished Queen Vashi.

Character Archetype

Ahasuerus takes on the literary character archetype of a Shapeshifter. This is a character that is unpredictable; he is one type of person in one moment and in the next moment he is someone completely different.

King Ahasuerus summons his lovely wife because he likes to behold her beauty. Moments later he banishes her forever, maybe even executes her. The literary function of the Shapeshifter is to add suspense to a story through uncertain behavior. It would be easy to write his behavior off in this scene to intoxication, but Ahasuerus continues his shapeshifting throughout the story. Right away, we learn we aren't sure what he will do next. The king is unpredictable.

Esther and The Gospel

Scene one in the first chapter of Esther gives a picture of one of the first scenes in the Bible between a husband and wife. Adam and Eve behaved badly, failing to protect each other, and failed to obey God. The result in Genesis chapter 3 was God putting a curse on Adam and Eve, hence all husbands and wives. Part of the curse on Adam and Eve was that husbands would rule over their wives, which is exactly what the king's decree asserts, that husbands would be masters over their wives. Results of the fall in Genesis and the fallout between the king and queen paint a picture of a never-ending conflict between husbands and wives. Their own desires became the idols they worshipped rather than worshipping the True, Living God.

Ahasuerus and Vashti both have dual character types that they reflect in chapter one. A character type in the Bible, or any other piece of literature, can have the function of pointing to another character, or acting as a symbol of another character.

Ahasuerus represents both a type of Adam and a type of husband. The sovereign king represents a type of God. As a type of Adam, he was not acting like a godly husband. Adam did not protect his wife, and his lack of protection led to her death. Likewise, Ahasuerus did not protect Vashti, and it led to her banishment and/or death, certainly a symbolic death. The events that transpired in the second half of chapter one point us to the events of chapter three in Genesis.

There are many occasions in the story of Esther that the king's position reflects a type of God's position. In this section of the story, as king, Ahasuerus is a sovereign ruler. He was the maker of laws that were immutable, laws that could not change. He was honor bound to follow through, even at significant cost to himself. The sovereign king reflects God's position as sovereign ruler of the universe. God's law dictates that sin separates us from God and rebellion carries a death penalty.

Queen Vashti represents a wife, like Eve, and she represents the bride of Christ, the Church. As Eve disobeyed her sovereign ruler, God, Vashti disobeys her king. Eve becomes mortal, and God banishes Adam and her from the Garden. They both become mortal and eventually die. The king banishes Vashti from the palace and she eventually dies. We, as Christ's bride, have the same death sentence as Eve. Vashti is a picture of it, a picture of the Church.

The 40,000-foot view of Esther chapter one gives us a picture of a vastly rich kingdom ruled by a king who has laws that cannot change and must be obeyed. We see an act of disobedience that leads to banishment and death. It is a re-telling of the story in the Garden of Eden. The first chapter of Esther reflects the first chapter of God's redemptive plan for his people, a people that need redemption and a people he loves enough to do whatever it takes to redeem them.

3
Esther 2:1-18

Context

The first eighteen verses of chapter two contain a lot of events that cover quite a bit of time. The text tells us that the king remembered what Vashti did and what he did in response. This scene depicts Vashti's absence, leaving the king without a queen. His attendants noticed the need to address the lack of companionship and suggested bringing young virgins to the king until he chose one to be his queen. We learn that there was quite an elaborate process to prepare the young women for their audition.

The writer introduces us to Mordecai and Esther, descendants of the Jews taken into captivity by Nebuchadnezzar of the Babylonian Empire. We learn that Mordecai is the older cousin who takes her in after her parent's death. As soon as we meet her, we learn she is a virgin who becomes a candidate to become queen, as she was very beautiful.

There was something extraordinary about Esther. She gained favor and special treatment from the eunuchs who prepared her, and Ahasuerus picked her out of all the other candidates to be his queen. He is so pleased with her that he prepared a huge celebration, gave gifts and a remission of taxes. This all takes place in the seventh year of his reign, four years after he dispensed with Queen Vashti.

Observations

Chapter 2 opens with the statement that after the king's anger abated, he remembered Vashti. The text does not give us an indication of how long it was after he kicked her to the curb, but it was likely a long time.

The story opens in the third year of his reign as king, and we find out later in this chapter that it was in the seventh year of his reign that Esther became queen. It is quite possible that it took months or even a year or two for Ahasuerus' anger to dissipate and miss his wife.

We all have been there. Someone offends us, deprives us of some right we think is ours, and we walk around for days, weeks or even years having an argument in our heads with the other person. We imagine a thousand ways to tell them how wrong they were in offending us. Sometimes we even follow through. Ahasuerus could hear Memucan's voice telling him how wrong Vashti was, and the king's pride gave him assurance that Vashti owed him her obedience. That is how it is with pride. It always assures us of our rights and other's obligations towards us.

Humankind has changed little in the 2,500 years since King Ahasuerus and Queen Vashti broke up. Marriages still break up over the simplest offense. Later, when anger subsides, when the divorce is long-since final, sometimes we realize that maybe the demands our pride made of us were far more costly than we ever dreamed. If only we could learn to swallow our pride and seek the best for our spouse, we might just find that we get what is best for us, too.

The day finally came, and Ahasuerus stopped listening to the angry voice of pride. In the quiet of his soul, with the loud voice of anger quelled, he heard the soft voice of his heart. He missed his wife. The text does not tell us so, but we can infer it from what the king's young men tell him. They must have realized that his heart was sad and lonely. Or maybe they realized that they could not do for the king what a wife could do for him.

In verse 2, we read, "Then the king's young men who attended him said, 'Let beautiful young virgins be sought out for the king.'" They were in close contact with him daily, so much so that they could see his heart ached and they had a strong inkling about what they should do. They presented the idea of a "Persia's Got Talent" search for the right girl to win the king's favor and the crown of the queen. The king liked the idea, and the search was on.

Meanwhile, back at the citadel, the narrative introduces us to Mordecai and Esther. Mordecai was Esther's older first cousin. Esther's parents had died, and Mordecai stepped in to raise her as his own daughter. We learn right away that they are Jews from the tribe of Benjamin. The author gives us a brief genealogy of Mordecai's decedents, recounting that his relatives were carried away from his homeland during the Babylonian captivity about 122 years earlier.

We also learn that Mordecai was a relative of Kish, a Benjaminite. Although it is uncertain if this Kish was the same one who was the father of King Saul, there is a strong possibility that it was the same person. This link to King Saul, the first king of Israel, serves as an essential footnote that connects our main and supporting protagonists to the historical lineage.

In chapter 24 of II Kings, we read that when Nebuchadnezzar, King of Babylon, conquered Jerusalem, he took 10,000 people captive. He took all the leaders, artisans, and anyone of value, leaving behind the poor people. For 122 years, Jews that were taken from Jerusalem made their homes in the Babylonian kingdom and subsequently in the Mede-Persian empire.

55 years before the story of Esther begins, in the third year of his reign, Cyrus had made a decree that allowed the Jews to return to Jerusalem. Some returned, but many had made their lives in the Persian kingdom. Mordecai and Esther were among the Jews that were content living among the pagan gentiles. Mordecai apparently had a position of some rank since he lived in the citadel, not somewhere else in the surrounding city. He must have not been eager to give up his social and/or political status, and he was possibly content keeping his Hebrew heritage private. His status seemed more important than his faith and identity as one of God's chosen people.

We can deduce that Mordecai was not keeping the ceremonial law and dietary restrictions, because those customs would quickly give him away as being Hebrew. For him to keep his heritage secret, he had to live like the Persians. He was not observing the law as a witness of his faith to those around him. If being a Jew was against the law, apparently there would not have been enough evidence to convict him.

The author introduces us to Esther as a Jew, and he adds she was beautiful to look at with a nice figure. Earlier, we were told that Vashti was beautiful to look at, but the text did not mention her figure. Hence, we can conclude that Esther had even better physical attributes than the former queen. So, when the decree went out to bring the most beautiful young virgins into the king's palace to be part of his harem, Esther would surely have known that she would be a prime candidate.

The text says nothing about how Esther came to be one of the young virgins that was taken into the king's harem. She may have answered an advertisement in the Persia Post or ventured into the town square to apply in person. Or maybe the king's men detained her at a checkpoint in town where officials took beautiful young virgins into custody. What we can conclude is that she did not go into hiding to avoid being taken into the harem. Nor did she rush and out and marry some young Hebrew boy and disqualify herself from consideration. She was, to a greater or lesser degree, complicit in participating in competition to be queen. She was willing to sleep with the king out of wedlock to win. Hence, Esther, like Mordecai, will relegate her faith to a secondary priority. The text does not clearly state that she was a willing contestant, not does it tell us she was unwilling. The writer leaves us to wonder.

Once authorities took Esther in as a prospect for becoming the king's wife, and consideration for filling the open queen position, they put her under the care of Hegai, the eunuch who was in charge of the harem. Mordecai advised her to keep her Hebrew heritage to herself, which she did. She gained favor with Hegai, and he gave her special care, along with seven of her own attendants. We therefore conclude that there was something extraordinary about Esther. Surely there were plenty of drop-dead, gorgeous women in the harem, but Esther had something more going for her.

Esther spent the next year preparing to meet the king. It was like being in an expensive beauty and health spa for a year. They gave her the best food, cosmetics, and skin treatments. As if she wasn't beautiful enough, she underwent a royal make-over that could make a silk purse out of a sow's ear. She must have been something marvelous to look at. I imagine there were a few lessons in etiquette too that prepared her to be in the king's company. I'll bet there was even a full lesson devoted to studying the decree that King Ahasuerus made regarding Queen Vashti!

When the customary year of beautification was complete, Esther had her turn to spend the night with the king. It would be a command performance, and there was only one chance, and one virginity, to give for the occasion. There could be one of three outcomes from the night with the king. The text says that after spending one night with the king, he would remand the contestant to her quarters with the other concubines. The best outcome would be to become queen. Second, a good performance might earn the reward of the king calling on her again, from time to time, to provide sexual service to the king. This could earn hers gifts and privileges. Third, a poor performance might leave a young maiden with nothing more than the chance to grow old alone with no hope of a husband. One might surmise that when the call came to have that special night with the king, the young virgin would employ whatever tools, tricks, or skills necessary to please the king. She would make every effort to improve her chances.

When Esther got the call, she took nothing with her except whatever Hegai suggested. She knew that substance over form would win the day, and her future. The text does not mention God at all in the book of Esther, but we see his providence in almost every verse. I believe that God's Holy Spirit worked in Esther to reveal to her what we read in I Peter 3:4, "but let your adorning be the hidden person of the heart with the imperishable beauty of a gentle and quiet spirit, which in God's sight is very precious." Whatever she did, it worked. Ahasuerus fell in love with Esther and made her queen, giving her the crown that once belonged to Vashti.

Literary Elements
Theme

The number seven as a literary theme continues from chapter 1 into chapter 2. We see it appear twice, first when Esther was given seven female attendants and second when Ahasuerus took her as his wife in the seventh year of his reign over Persia. Again, the number seven reminds us of the seven days of creation, as an affirmation that this king, his palace, his servants and all the splendors are complete. The good bride, the good bridegroom, and the wedding feast point us to the marriage supper of the lamb.

Mood

The mood of this chapter picks up where chapter one leaves off, with a mood of legalism and separation due to transgression of the law. Yet, we quickly transition to a mood of grace, favor, and acceptance that continues throughout the chapter. As we will see in subsequent chapters and scenes, the shifting from a mood of legalism to grace occurs repeatedly. It is a picture of our Christian walk. We face the continual paradox of God's law and his infinite grace that save us from the consequences of the law. As believers, all of us experience the cycle of conviction of sin that drives us to faith in Jesus. Let us hope that we never get so comfortable with the saving grace of God that we forget we are called to repent from our sins.

The mood shift also points us to, among other passages, Ephesians 1:4, "even as He chose us in Him before the foundation of the world, that we should be holy and blameless before Him." Esther, like Christ's bride, was chosen, made holy, blameless, and accepted.

Story Structure

In the story structure of The Hero's Journey, we see Esther progress through the first few stages in the first half of chapter two. Stage 1 is *the ordinary world*. The author introduces Esther as a beautiful, young, Hebrew woman living with her older cousin in Susa. Her parents were dead, and her older cousin took her in as his own daughter. This was her ordinary world. We learn little about it beyond that.

Stage 2, *the call to adventure*, arises when the king began a search for a new wife. The text does not tell us how she received the call, whether it was by hearing about the search and answering the call, or if it the king's men found her and took her. The call may have been voluntary or involuntary.

If it was voluntary, one might conjecture that she thought about it and had some fear and hesitation telling her to refuse the call. If she refused the call, she would linger in the stage of the *refusal of the call*. She may have refused the call at first, but eventually she entered the competition. If they took her involuntarily, she may have refused the call in her heart. Either way, there is a strong possibility that the third stage of the Hero's Journey, *refusal of the call*, happened. Whatever the case, a refusal of the call was not germane to this story.

Stage 4, *meeting with a mentor* happens as well. Esther actually has two mentors, Mordecai and Hegai, the eunuch in charge of the women. Mordecai gave her the advice to not reveal that she was a Hebrew. Esther gained favor with Hegai and he took her under his wing as a favored contestant. We learn later that he gave her wise advice.

Stage 5 is *crossing the first threshold*. This is when Esther spends the first night with the king. How scary that must have been! She had prepared for this night for a full year. During that time, she saw one young virgin after another go to the king's chambers, only to end up in the custody of the eunuch who cared for concubines. Think about how much temptation there could have been to run away, but she didn't. She went to the king with such a demeanor that the king fell head over heels for her.

The limited text does not unpack for us all that Esther thought or did during the events in chapter 2. We can suspect that there was a lot of fear, doubt, and second guessing. After all, the Hebrews were aliens in Susa, sojourners in a foreign land. They are God's chosen people living among gentile heathens. She may have speculated about what extent to which a good Hebrew boy or girl should embrace the worldly ways of the Persians.

Like Daniel, many of the Jews likely would have refused to eat their food, drink their wine, go to their movies, listen to their music, or even have a meal with them, metaphorically speaking. Think about us as Christians today. In many Christian circles, it is not acceptable to eat certain foods, go to worldly movies, hang out with non-Christian friends, or even work with a non-Christian who misbehaves. I have two friends that I know of who quit high-level jobs because a co-worker was having an affair. They felt that workplace association with them constituted approval of their life choices. Such conflicts over being in the world, but not of the world, are as old as our faith itself.

For whatever reason, Esther chose to enter a world, a world of heathens, godless kings, eunuchs, and concubines. Living in a challenging world where virgin girls faced a life of lavish wealth or loneliness couldn't have been easy for her, but it was the place God had put her in. Recognizing an opportunity to alter the status quo, she bravely entered a completely new realm.

Esther and The Gospel

We know that Christ's work on the cross makes his bride acceptable and beautiful. It is not anything we can do for ourselves. Without God's regeneration, we are ugly, filthy sinners, unworthy to be in God's presence. The year Esther spent in beautification treatments ordered and paid for by the king is a picture of the king paying the price for making Esther beautiful and acceptable. Christ made us, his bride, beautiful and acceptable. This is where Esther portrays a type of bride, the bride of Christ.

In verse eighteen, we read, "Then the king gave a grand feast for all his officials and servants; it was Esther's feast. He also granted a remission of taxes to the provinces and gave gifts with royal generosity." In this verse, we see a picture of the wedding feast of the Lamb, where the elect unites with Christ in heaven. It will be a glorious celebration in which God lavishes gifts on us with royal generosity.

We also see that Ahasuerus presents the picture of a true, good husband. He gives a feast for Esther and rejoices over his bride. Contrast this to the celebration feast described in chapter 1, which was not Vashti's feast, rather the king left her out and she had to provide one of her own. In chapter one, we saw a picture of Adam and Eve in the garden. They received a curse on their marriage after they rebelled, a curse that extends to all humankind. In chapter two, we see a picture of redemption.

4

Esther 2:19-23

Context

Esther 2:19 reads, "Now when the virgins were gathered together the second time, Mordecai was sitting at the king's gate." The king's gate was the only entrance and exit to the palace compound. Archeological excavation revealed that the gate to the palace in Susa was an enormous brick structure, much larger than a three-story house. The gate itself was possibly forty feet high. There was a moat around the palace and a bridge over the moat ended at the king's gate.

The gate would have been one of the most significant places in Susa. It is the place where the king would give and receive communication with the people. It is the place where the citizens would come to communicate with the king, either bringing their requests, or their complaints. The king would station guards there for protection and palace officials to serve as the conduit for incoming and outflowing communication. For Mordecai to be sitting in the king's gate, he must have held some sort of official position in the capital. It was not likely a place where they would allow loitering.

There is no explanation of who the virgins were and the occasion of gathering them together for the second time. The text does not provide any instructive context of Mordecai sitting in the king's gate other than suggesting that he held a position that called for him to be there. At first blush, there does not seem to be a reason for mentioning the second gathering of virgins, yet there is always a reason for including information in the canon of scripture.

Observations

One explanation might be that after the king went through the first gathering of virgins and chose Esther to be queen, he found the practice of sampling the companionship of a long parade of virgins to be a pleasant thing to do. He may have continued by having a second round of virgin-gathering, even after having chosen a new queen. It was not uncommon for kings of that day to have many wives and concubines. Even the Hebrew kings like David and Solomon had more than one wife.

Later, in chapter 4, we learn that there was a period of 30 days in which the king had not called Esther to see him or be with him. This seems to be a long time for a king to go without the intimate company of a beautiful young wife, unless the king was entertaining the company of other women. Maybe the reason the writer included this bit of information is for the reader to consider it in chapter 4 rather than chapter 2. We will get to that in our exploration of Esther chapter 4.

Verse 20 discloses that Esther had obeyed the command of Mordecai to not disclose being Hebrew to the king or to anyone else. This serves to instruct the reader about the character of Esther. She was obedient to Mordecai as unto a father, even though he was not her father. After all, he was in a position of authority over her. Esther continues to be obedient to Mordecai's instruction, even after she became queen.

Yet, this obedience reveals something less savory about her character. She hid her identity as a Hebrew, which meant that she had to hide the practices of her faith. Esther did not pray in a way that revealed her as a Hebrew, nor did she take sacrifices to the local temple. Esther did not practice the rituals surrounding uncleanliness and cleansing. In short, she compromised her obedience to God. Yet God uses her nonetheless to save his people.

It was while sitting in the gate that Mordecai learned of a plot by two eunuchs to lay hands on King Ahasuerus. We do not know the nature of the plot, but it is easy to imagine the anger and bitterness that could lead to making such a plot. Such powerful men that worked as guards could have enjoyed great power and respect if they had remained whole men instead of being gelded. It is also quite possible that they were men who were formerly citizens of a conquered nation, like Israel. Whatever the reasons, there could have been many reasons for them to want to do harm to Ahasuerus. After all, King Ahasuerus was prone to rash and unjust decisions.

This short account of the two eunuchs' plot and their subsequent hanging does not have as much importance here as it does in chapter six when the king remembers the incident. Again, we will come to that in due time, but the details of the story mentioned here are of great importance later.

In just a few short verses, we read about two pieces of information that do not become important until later in the story. We must interpret them in light of the scripture verses that follow, and the interpretation is this: God providentially orders and plans all things for the good of his people. The text never mentions God in book of Esther, but his handiworks are on continual display.

Literary Elements
Theme

Despite the vestiges of the old, sinful man being on display, God uses the gathering of more virgins for King Ahasuerus as part of his grand plan for Esther to fulfill her destiny as a hero. God also uses the plot by the eunuchs to bring harm to the king as part of his grand plan, to not only save Mordecai but make him a hero too. This emerges as a theme in this chapter. God is always preparing something good for his people, even when we do not see it or are aware of it.

Mood

In the first 18 verses of chapter 2, we saw the mood open as one of legalism and shift to one of grace. In the concluding verses, we see the mood and make another interesting shift. Our response to God's grace should be one of doing what is right, considering how gracious he has been to us. Here we see Mordecai and Esther do what is right towards the king by exposing a plot to hurt him. This is an appropriate response. As a result, the two men who plotted to lay hands on the king received a death sentence. The mood shifts to one of justice. As observers, we get a sense of justice and well-being from knowing that God punishes evil men. This points to the fact that we, as Christians, enjoy the same mood of justice, knowing that God has just judgment in store for those who plot evil.

Story Structure

The next stage of the Hero's Journey is *tests, allies, and enemies*. In this stage, our heroine encounters people that help her as allies, people who pose a threat to her as enemies, and tests that challenge her character, commitment, and endurance. Mordecai continues to be her ally in that he exposes the plot to kill the king. If the two guards killed the king, that would be the end of Esther's heroine journey. Bigthan and Teresh, the two eunuchs, emerge as enemies of the king and our heroine. We can deduce that the gathering of a second set of virgins would pose a significant test for Esther. Such a situation certainly would introduce insecurity into the marriage. And as we learn later, the king ignores her for thirty days, which causes her to have a fear of approaching him.

Esther also undergoes a test to see what she will do with the information she gets from Mordecai. Imagine if you were in her shoes. Her husband has been bringing more virgins into the palace and spending time with them, possibly having sexual relations. Think of the hurt she must have felt. Then she learns there is a plot to kill him. There could have been no small temptation to just keep it secret and let the deed go down. She passes the test with flying colors, showing her allegiance to her king. She protects her husband from the plot of his enemies.

Archetypes

Bigthan and Teresh are shadow archetypes that serve many functions in the story, creating a more dynamic plot and adding conflict. They set up Mordecai to become a hero archetype. Both Mordecai and Esther serve the archetype of a herald; they bring the news of a plot to the king.

Esther and the Gospel

In the final scene of chapter two, Esther portrays a type of bride. This is not a literary archetype, rather it is a Biblical character type that she pictures. When the serpent approached Eve in the Garden of Eden, he deceived her and convinced her to do something that would bring death to her and her husband. She ate the fruit and gave it to him to eat. Thereby, she played a part in the fall of humankind. Adam should have intervened and protected her and thereby was more at fault because of the position God gave him. Adam and Eve became mortal, doomed to die in the flesh. God also banished them from the garden, which represents his kingdom. From that point forward, they and all their progeny would require the intercession of a savior, Jesus, to be in communion with God again. Even though Jesus would not make atonement for their sins until thousands of years later, God made them acceptable by what Jesus would do.

In this situation, Esther portrays an exemplary bride and protects her husband from the threat of death. She portrays the type of bride that we, as the Church, are called to be, faithful to our bridegroom, Jesus Christ. In Romans chapter five and First Corinthians chapter 15, the texts speak of Christ as being the Second Adam by redeeming the sin nature that comes to us from the first Adam. Similarly, the Church, the second Eve, becomes obedient through Christ's justifying work on the cross. Esther points us to that wonderful redemption Jesus imputes to his bride.

5

Esther 3

Context

In verse one of chapter three, we learn that King Ahasuerus appointed Haman the Agagite to be on a throne over all the officials of his kingdom. It is noteworthy to observe that the writer of the book of Esther, maybe Mordecai, guided by God's Holy Spirit, told us that Haman was an Agagite. The writer did not recount Haman's resume of accomplishments, he did not give us his previous title as an official in the kingdom, nor did he give any account of some extraordinary deed that gained him the promotion. All the text tells us is that he is an Agagite, and it is the only piece of information about Haman that is important to the big picture of the story.

Being an Agagite shows Haman was a descendant of Agag, who was king of the Amalekites during the reign of King Saul, King of Israel. The story of Agag and the Amalekites is central to the events that unfold in Esther. In I Samuel 15:2-3, we read, "Thus says the Lord of hosts, 'I have noted what Amalek did to Israel in opposing them on the way when they came up out of Egypt. Now go and strike Amalek and devote to destruction all that they have. Do not spare them, but kill both man and woman, child and infant, ox and sheep, camel, and donkey.'"

Saul did as the God commanded by attacking the Amalekites, but when he defeated them, he did not devote everything to destruction. He killed the people, but he spared King Agag. Although I cannot be sure, I suspect this was an act of pride to keep a defeated king under his rule. He also spared all the livestock. Since we know Haman is a descendent of Agag, we can conclude that Saul must have spared Agag's family, too. The existence of Haman as an Agagite and an Amalekite tells us something about Haman, something about God and something about Mordecai. We will unpack these tidbits as we work through the text.

Upon promoting Haman to be over all the officials of Persia, Ahasuerus signed a decree that all the servants at the king's gate must bow down and pay homage to Haman. Mordecai, who apparently had a position that put him at the king's gate regularly, did not bow down and pay homage to Haman. Others at the gate asked Mordecai why he did not bow down, and he answered them by saying it was because he was a Jew. This is the only information the text gives us as to why Mordecai would not bow down and pay homage.

Observations

Most likely, Mordecai's refusal to pay homage was because there was enmity between the Amalekites and the Israelites. Similar to the Hatfields and the McCoys, there was bad blood between these two people groups that went back for many generations.

When Haman learned Mordecai would not pay homage, he became enraged. Yet he did not follow the same course of action as King Darius did in Daniel chapter 6. Daniel had continued to bow down and worship the God of Israel during a time when Darius decreed no one would worship any god but him for 30 days. When he found out that Daniel was worshiping his God, he gave the order to throw him in the lion's den. It was not enough for Haman to execute Mordecai, but he wanted to exact vengeance on all the Hebrews. The text says he disdained to only lay hands-on Mordecai, and he sought to destroy all the Jews. He saw it as an opportunity to wipe out the enemies of his ancestors.

Hence, Haman reveals himself to be a type of the antichrist. Throughout history, the spirit of the antichrist has sought to destroy

God's chosen people from the face of the earth. The spirit of the antichrist, as a serpent in the Garden of Eden, sought to destroy God's children by luring Adam and Eve into sin, knowing they would surely die if they ate of the fruit of the forbidden tree. He deceived them into eating.

In Egypt, the spirit of the antichrist came upon Pharaoh and induced him to kill all the babies and throw them into the river. At the time of Jesus' birth, Herod ordered the execution of all male babies. Hitler acted through the influence of the spirit of the antichrist to destroy all the Jews in Europe, and Hitler would have done it throughout the world if allied forces had not defeated him. It is a theme we see running the entire course of human history; the antichrist wants to rob God of His kingdom and children. Haman's act represents the ongoing conflict between God's elect and the devil, a microcosm of the larger conflict.

Haman used the occasion to destroy the Jews. Yet, he was unsure about the timing of it. So, he cast lots, or pur, to see when to carry out his evil plan. They cast pur for 12 months before Haman believed that casting pur would give him the most opportune time and date to carry out the death sentence for the Jews.

Literary Elements
Theme

We see several themes in this chapter that all pertain to measuring of time and the fullness of time. The numbers twelve and thirteen appear several times. When Haman became enraged by Mordecai, he cast pur in the first month of the year, the month of Nisan. This began in the twelfth year of the king's reign. The text tells us that "they" cast pur every day, all year long, until the twelfth month of the year, Adar. Haman used the of casting pur to determine the date when he would annihilate the Jews. The twelve-month long pur casting represents completeness.

Pur casting revealed that they should destroy the Jews in the twelfth month of the following year, which would be the thirteenth year of the king's reign. On the thirteenth day of the first month of the following year, they summoned the king's scribes to write the decree in every language that they would destroy the Jews on the thirteenth day of the twelfth month of the year. Hence, from the time Haman took out his revenge on the Jews to the appointed day of the annihilation would be a complete 24-month period, two complete years. And the number thirteen appears to be very *unlucky* for the Jews.

Mood

Verses ten though fifteen give us some of some details about the new decree that Ahasuerus put out, condemning the Jews to death. We read about the signet ring, the decree, kingdom officials, and sealed letters sent to all provinces. These details reveal the seriousness of the new law and they set up the mood of legalism, which reflects the legalism that permeates the Old Testament books of the law. The mood lands on us with heavy force. We can only conclude that one does not trifle with the king, which represents the parallel fact that one should not trifle with God. His laws are serious, all-encompassing, and immutable. They stretch into every corner of the kingdom and there is no place one can go to escape the law. The law was given in every language and script, showing that ignorance of the law was no excuse. The implications of the law created a heavy mood.

Story Structure

We chronicled the first five stages of The Hero's Journey, leading to Esther crossing the first threshold, in which Esther went to be with the king. We witnessed the beginning of the sixth stage of the journey called, *tests, allies, and enemies,* in which our hero encounters a series of tests that reveal courage, character, and strength, or maybe the lack thereof. Our sixth stage of the Hero's Journey continues in Esther chapter three. She encounters more tests, allies, and enemies. The literary function of this stage is multi-faceted. Events of this stage almost always raise the stakes for our hero, and they provide conflict, drama, and tension. These events will slowly build the story to a powerful climax in which our heroine undergoes the ultimate test that makes or breaks her. In chapter three, Haman becomes an enemy of the heroine, and the test is one of facing certain death, not only for our heroine, but for all of her people.

From a story point of view, Esther 1 & 2 make up act I of the story. The first act, in literary function, is the set-up of the story and introduces the plot. Act II is the introduction of the conflict and confrontation between the protagonist and the antagonist. In Esther, act two begins with chapter 3 and ends in chapter four. The storm clouds are forming, and doom and gloom are on the horizon. We know what the stakes are, and they are high. Given the precedent that no one can revoke the decrees of a Persian king, we have a story worthy problem that leaves the reader wondering how in the world we are going to arrive at a happy ending. In human terms, it is an impossible situation. Israel is going to die. But God has a plan. He is not in heaven wringing his hands, wondering what to do. Matthew 19:26 says, "But Jesus looked at them and said, 'With man this is impossible, but with God all things are possible.'" Even though the book of Esther never mentions God, He is about to show up!

Character Archetypes

We see several character archetypes in this chapter. Haman is a picture of the antichrist, but The Hero's Journey model calls this a Shadow character archetype. The Shadow archetype is very close to, if not the same as an antichrist figure in that the Shadow represents darkness, evil or something sinister. In many stories, the Shadow is the antagonist or the right-hand man to the antagonist.

Another archetype we see throughout the story of Esther is the Shapeshifter, which is a character that continually keeps the hero (and us as readers) off balance by changing in unpredictable ways. Ahasuerus is a Shapeshifter in that he makes rash, unpredictable decisions. He, as a matter of course, asks his advisors what to do, and he makes decisions with little forethought about the end results. In chapter 3, his decision based on Haman's request condemns an entire race to destruction, and there is no evidence that he asked a second advisor about it. There is no evidence that he thought about how much he would lose in tax revenue from the Jews after he killed them all. He did not count the costs. And it is obvious he did not consult his bride of 5 years about what to do!

Setting

The events in this chapter occur, and linger at the king's gate, and then shift to the king's throne room. The king's gate is the entry to the king's palace, and into his presence. This is a picture of the gates of heaven. Revelation 21:21 describes the gates of heaven. "And the 12 gates were 12 pearls, each of the gates made of a single pearl, and the street of the city was pure gold, transparent as glass." This is where we get our modern reference to the pearly gates. In both cases, one must enter through a gate to come into the presence of a sovereign.

Esther and the Gospel

When Haman presented his plot to King Ahasuerus for approval, he told a story about one man's rebellion to implicate all Jews in order to convince Ahasuerus to agree to his proposed genocide. In verse 8, he tells the king, "There is a certain people scattered abroad and dispersed among the peoples in all the provinces of your kingdom. Their laws are different than every other people, and they do not keep the king's law." In reality there was only one Jew who would not keep just one of the king's laws. Mordecai was the one and only person who would not keep the law by bowing down and paying homage to Haman.

So, one man disobeying the law became the reason for all the Jews to get a death sentence. Sound familiar? Remember Adam in the garden? In speaking of Adam, Paul tells us in Romans 5:12, "Therefor, just as sin came into the world through one man, and death through sin, so death spread to all men because all sinned..." Adam was our federal head whose sin contaminated us all with a sin nature.

Here, Mordecai becomes the picture of Adam, our federal head, who brought death to us all. Haman is a type of the antichrist, as an accuser of the brethren. He also was second in rank Persia to the king. As such, Haman pictures Satan who was second to God in heaven before God cast him out upon his rebellion. The king as a sovereign ruler provides a picture of God who cannot tolerate rebellion. We will see these character types continue into the following chapters, providing pictures of God, Satan, and Adam.

In Esther's time, God's covenant family was the Jewish nation. Sin and death were hanging over their heads like the Sword of Damocles. They desperately needed a savior. The chapter ends with a cliffhanger like a modern television show. Haman and Ahasuerus sit down to drink, toasting to the destruction of the Jews, but the death declaration threw the city into confusion and desperation. Like us, the Jews were undone without a savior. The king had condemned our heroine and her people. If this were a television series, the narrator would say, "Be sure to tune in next week to see what happens to Esther, Mordecai and all the Jews!"

6

Esther 4

Context

Chapter 4 begins with the account of Mordecai's response to the king's decree regarding the fate of the Jews. He tore his clothes and went into the city to cry out in a "loud and bitter cry". We would respond the same way if it were culturally acceptable behavior. Putting on sackcloth and ashes was a fitting response to bad news for the Jews. Yet, this response begs for answers to several questions.

The location for Mordecai's crying out was the king's gate. This is the third time in as many chapters that the scene took place at the king's gate. Nothing in scripture is irrelevant. There must be a special significance to this location of wailing. We will get to that in my observations.

Communication between Esther and Mordecai only took place through messengers. The text tells us that no one wearing sack cloth could pass through the king's gate, and Esther did not go out to see him. In fact, the news of Mordecai's actions came to Esther through her young women and Eunuchs. When she heard about his loud and bitter cries, she sent clothes and messages to him to stop, and he replied to her through the messengers. There was no face-to-face contact between them.

Apparently, news about the degree had not reached Esther and Mordecai had to send news and a copy of the written decree to her through the messengers. Esther explained why she dared not see the king, but Mordecai insisted the king would not spare her. He made it clear that he believed she providentially was in the palace for such a time as this.

Observations

First, who was Mordecai crying out to in a "loud and bitter cry?" For devout Jews of that day, the cry would have been to God. The text does not mention crying out to God. In fact, the scene and location of his crying out reveal that Mordecai went to the king's gate to put on his public display of mourning. Could this have been a sad testimony to Mordecai's faith? Apparently, he was crying out so the king would hear him. I am not casting stones at Mordecai because I have done similar acts on many occasions. It is our nature to take a horizontal view of our problems and solutions rather than a vertical one. All too often, we take our eyes off God.

Esther got news of his actions and sent him clothes so that he would stop bringing attention to himself. He would have nothing of it. He wanted to be noticed by the king. When his behavior did not yield the results he wanted, he tried to enlist Esther to go speak to the king. Mordecai may have been putting his trust in the king, not in God. The text does not tell us. Nonetheless, I will give him the benefit of the doubt and believe he trusted in God while he was working in his temporal world to effect a change.

When I worked as a missionary, we often repeated the saying, "Work like it all depends on you, and pray like it all depends on God." I have often reflected on whether this saying is theologically correct, but it does somewhat echo Proverbs 21:31, "The horse is prepared for the day of battle, but the victory is of the Lord." This Proverb suggests we should do the things that are in our power but put our trust in God. Let's hope that is what Mordecai was doing here.

I do not want to read too much into the story that does not come to us through the text, but let the text tell us what happened. Mordecai does not mention trusting in God for the outcome of this situation. He does not even mention the need for prayer. He takes action that would get the king's attention by mourning at his gate. When this effort failed, he sent word to Esther for her to go to the king and make an appeal for her people.

Esther's response tells us several important things about the king, about God and about herself. First, she replies saying that no one may go into the inner chamber to see the king without him summoning them. Such an act may cause an immediate death sentence. If one went to the king uninvited, the king might grant them favor with a motion of his royal scepter. One does not trifle with the King of Persia! No one may come into his presence unless he deems them worthy. This informs us about what the risk is of going to see the king without a summons. It tells us that even Esther does not have a free pass to see His Majesty when she wants to.

The second thing we learn from Esther's response is that she has not been called in to see the king in the past 30 days. The temporal reason for this could be that the king was occupied with spending the night with other virgins. Her suspicion, although not directly said, is that she does not feel like she is in the king's favor. She has not heard from him or seen him lately, and it could have felt to her like he does not need or want her anymore.

Esther told Mordecai why she was afraid to go into the king's chamber. Mordecai affirmed her fears when he told her that the king would not spare her. Again, this points to the fact that no one could come into the presence of God without the work of an intercessor.

Mordecai tells her by messenger, "And who knows whether you have not come into the kingdom for such a time as this?" This statement comes as close as we get in all ten chapters of Ester to say she is part of God's providential plan to save his chosen people. The text does not mention providence, but it implies it. There is a glimmer of faith in Mordecai, and we see it in this crisis.

Esther calls for her people to fast with her for three days. After that time, she would go see the king uninvited. She says, "...if I perish, I perish." She acknowledges she is a condemned person, and that she is completely reliant upon the king's mercy for her life and the life of her people.

Literary Elements
Theme

The literary theme of legalism, judgement, and death return in chapter 4. We left chapter 3 with the decree going out to all the land that the Hebrews must die. The heaviness of this decree clings to us throughout this chapter. For the Jews in Persia, it was an inescapable heaviness, and it points to the inescapable heaviness for us all, that the wages of sin are death. If one wants to consider the wages of sin, look no further than the first twelve chapters of Joshua. There we see God execute judgment on the Amorites for their sin. He commands Joshua to put them all to death. Mordecai's sin against Haman led to the death sentence for all of God's chosen people, just as Adam's sin led to a death sentence for us all. It was not good news.

The overarching theme of the story of Esther is God's providence, and it provides hope for us. Even when we do not see him at work, even when we do not feel loved by him, even when we are not praying and relying on Him, God is at work for our good in the spiritual realm. Our salvation does not depend on us, on our prayers, on our fasting or any other works. God has done for us what we could never do for ourselves by providing the perfect mediator, the perfect priest to intercede for us, Jesus. This whole story points to Jesus. And just as Mordecai and Esther did not live sold-out lives for God, a merciful God had a plan to save them. He has a plan for us, too.

A second theme in this chapter is when Esther ordered three times that something be done. She orders the eunuch to give Mordecai clothes to wear. She orders him to take a message. And the chapter ends with a statement saying that he obeyed her orders. Verse 17 says, "Mordecai then went away and did everything as Esther had ordered him." This marks a transition for her from portraying a type of bride to becoming a type of hero, a type of Christ, a picture that will grow in the following chapters. She is not taking orders any longer, she is giving them.

Mood

The literary mood of this chapter is one of mourning, one of hopelessness. This chapter paints the picture of the darkest hour just before dawn. It all looks bleak for our Hebrew forerunners. The edict threw the capital of Susa into confusion and our heroes jump on the treadmill of their feeble works to save themselves. The narrator of this story shows us how lost the Hebrews are. They are on death row, awaiting the day of execution.

Story Structure

This chapter marks Esther's entry into the seventh stage of The Hero's Journey, *approach to the inmost cave*. It is the stage in which heroes face the fact that their destiny is about to take them into a dark place where evil and death await. This stage is one in which there typically is a threshold that the hero must cross and there will be a threshold guardian that tries to prevent the hero from crossing. Jesus' approach to the inmost cave covered about a week in time. It began with the Triumphal Entry. To many around him, it may have looked like he had entered his glory, but he knew what awaited him at the end of the week. The threshold that he had to cross was his arrest and trial. His threshold guardian was Peter, who cut off the guard's ear when they came to arrest Jesus.

Peter did not want him to cross the threshold because he did not understand God's plan. Knowing the pain and agony he faced in the flesh would already have been a deterrent for Jesus to crossing over the threshold. Jesus knew that he would have to die a horrible death, descend into hell and an actual cave, the burial chamber. Even worse, Jesus had to bear his father's wrath for our sin. It was an agonizing realization that led to him sweating actual blood while in Gethsemane.

Esther tried to turn back from this stage of her journey, but Mordecai convinced her to press ahead. Her threshold guardian was not an actual person, rather a circumstance. The king had not called her in to be with him in thirty days. This made her feel unwelcome and more at risk of him having her put to death. After all, she surely knew what fate befell Queen Vashti. At last, she said, "if I perish, I perish," but in the quiet hours, during the watches of the nights, you can imagine that she was exceedingly afraid Yet, she did not turn back, did not waiver, and did not fail. She did what heroines do, pushed through her fear, crossed the threshold.

Archetypes

When Mordecai sent word to Esther about the decree, even sending her a hard copy, he fulfilled the character archetype of Herald. He gave her the call that was upon her life. Further, he continued as the archetype of her mentor by encouraging her about what she must do. Even during this seismic shift of Esther transforming into a leader, one giving orders, Mordecai was still her mentor.

Esther and the Gospel

As we have seen in the previous chapters of Esther, there is a dichotomy between what is transpiring in human terms and foundational kingdom principals that the events represent. I was a little hard on dear Mordecai about his response to the decree. He turned to the king for help, first by trying to draw attention to himself and then by appealing to Esther to go see the king. It looked as though he was putting his trust in man, not God.

Yet, the sovereign king, Esther, Mordecai, and Haman are pictures of God, Christ, the Church, and Satan, depending on the scene. Here, when Mordecai goes to the king's gate to cry out, it is a picture of how the Church needs to go to the throne of God to cry out for our help. As I previously mentioned, the king's gate was where the people could bring their petitions and communication to the king. For us as believers, we bring our petitions to the throne room of God.

Esther sent word to Mordecai about the risk of going to see the king. She told him that seeing him could carry a death sentence unless the king gives mercy by holding out his royal scepter. While this law reveals something to us about the Persian king, it also reminds us of the divine nature of our God. When God gave Moses the design of the tabernacle and the laws of the tabernacle, he decreed no one could enter the Holy of Holies or they would die. Only the high priest, the chosen intercessor between man and God, could go in, and even then, only once a year after sacrificing for the atonement of sin.

This law regarding the Holy of Holies points to Christ as the perfect intercessor who will stand before God on our behalf. The story of Esther and the king points to the same reference point, Christ, our Holy Priest forever. He is the only one who can stand in the presence of a perfect God and plead on our behalf. Later, when Esther goes into the king's chamber, she fills the role of a type of Christ, standing in the gap for all of God's chosen people.

As I mentioned before, Mordecai's statement to Esther was, "And who knows whether you have not come into the kingdom for such a time as this?" Esther here portrays a type of Jesus. If you recall Jesus' words after the triumphal entry, as he approached his threshold, when he said, "Now is my soul troubled. And what shall I say? 'Father, save me from this hour?' But for this purpose, I have come to this hour. Father, glorify your name." Then a voice came from heaven: "I have glorified it, and I will glorify it again." (John 12: 27, 28) The stage of Esther's and Jesus' Hero's Journey are parallel and the words are too similar to miss the symbolism. Esther must answer the call to save her people, just as Jesus did roughly six hundred years later.

7

Esther 5

Context

Chapter five verse one says, "On the third day, Esther put on her royal robes and stood in the inner court of the king's palace." We read that the king finds favor in her and he admits her into his throne room. Esther had completed the three days of fasting; she conquered her fear of the death penalty and found success by gaining the king's acceptance. The king responds favorably to Esther and offers her anything she wants, up to half the kingdom.

Her request is for the king and Haman to come to a feast she prepared for them. Ahasuerus and Haman came to the feast, and again, he offered her anything up to half the kingdom. A second time, she asked for the two of them to come to another feast on the next day. The king accepted, and Haman was giddy with excitement.

At the gate, after leaving Esther's feast, Haman encounters Mordecai, who does not pay homage. Haman was infuriated and went home to complain to family and friends. They convinced him to build gallows and ask the king to have Mordecai hanged the next morning.

Observations

When the king admitted Esther into his throne room, Ahasuerus asked her what he could do for her. He said he would give to her up to half of his kingdom. The king switched from being a picture of a sovereign ruler to being a type of husband. Only this time, he was not a type of bad husband, as he was in chapter one. This new husband is a type of husband that God created men to be. The king declared that he would share up to half of his kingdom with his bride. This illustrates the truth that wives are equal heirs with their husbands in the kingdom of heaven. "Likewise, husbands, live with your wives in an understanding way, showing honor to the woman as the weaker vessel, since they are heirs with you of the grace of life, so that your prayers may not be hindered." I Peter 3:17. In one brief scene, we see references to several kingdom truths: Christ denied his flesh to the point of death, God made us acceptable, and husbands and wives are equal heirs to the kingdom of heaven.

Esther delays in making her request known to the king and asks for Haman and him to come to a feast that she will prepare. When they come together, the characters they represent portray symbolic figures in God's redemptive plan for his people. The sovereign king is symbolic of God, the sovereign ruler and Haman is symbolic of Satan, Esther portrays a type of Christ, and Mordecai, sitting at the king's gate, represents the Church.

On the day of the feast, the king again offers Esther whatever she wants, up to half of his kingdom. This time, she stalls and asks the king and Haman to come to another feast the next day. It is not clear in the text what she is up to, but God is providentially at work to create suspense with the king, and maybe making it harder for him to say no to her request. Whatever the case, it creates a day of waiting in which we encounter two scenes that thicken the plot.

Haman leaves the palace and encounters Mordecai, who refuses to pay homage to him again. This infuriates Haman, who goes home and recounts all his wealth and grandeur to his friends and family to enlist their agreement that he deserves homage. His pride reached its fullest, right before his fall. Does this remind you of anyone?

Isaiah 14:12-15 says, "How you have fallen from heaven, O Day Star, son of Dawn! How you are cut down to the ground, you who laid the nations low! You said in your heart, 'I will ascend to heaven; above the stars of God I will set my throne on high; I will sit on the mount of assembly in the far reaches of the north; I will ascend above the heights of the clouds; I will make myself like the Most High.' But you are brought down to Sheol, to the far reaches of the pit." This passage is an account of Satan rebelling against God, and we see Haman as a symbol of Satan. I imagine that his account of his own splendor to his family sounded much like Satan describing his splendor in the passage above. Proverbs 16:18 says, "Pride goes before destruction, and a haughty spirit before a fall." Spoiler alert, Haman's pride and boasting are elements of foreshadowing.

Haman's wife and friends console him about Mordecai and convince him to build a gallows fifty cubits high on which to hang Mordecai the next morning. He thinks this is a splendid idea and orders his people to build the gallows. I imagine he went to bed that night quite pleased with his idea of putting an end to his enemy. In fact, I imagine his delight was a lot like Satan's as he made plans to hang Jesus on a cross. To Satan's dismay, the cross would be his undoing instead. Likewise, and symbolically, the gallows is the instrument of the undoing of Haman, a picture of Satan.

Literary Elements
Theme

Chapter four ended with a reference to Esther calling on the Jews to fast for three days and nights. Chapter five begins with, "On the third day Esther put on her royal robes and stood in the inner court of the king." The number three becomes a theme that causes us to think of other occasions that the number was significant. Esther denies herself for three days, which alludes to Christ's denial of himself for three days when he descended into hell. This is similar to the picture of Jonah spending three days in the belly of a fish.

Mood

The mood of this chapter shifts again to grace. It is the second time that we see a mood of legalism and heaviness shift to hope and grace. Is this not a lot like the course of a Christian life? Paul reminds the believers in Galatia that if they are trusting in how they follow the Law to achieve their sanctification, that it will end in bitter disappointment (Galatians chapter 3) Similarly, the accuser of the brethren likes to remind us we deserve death, but the Holy Spirit reminds us that Jesus gives us life. Our story, indeed, our whole life, is a microcosm of this great duality. Our moods often swing from legalistic despair over our sin to joy over God's grace. Christ has already perfected us, but not yet. For a while, we must live in the flesh with hope.

Story Structure

This chapter brings us to the 8th stage of The Hero's Journey, *the ordeal*. This is the stage in which the hero either dies for a cause, faces death, or accepts he will die to achieve a greater good. In Esther's case, she is willing to give up her life for the cause of saving her people. She lays it all on the line when she appears before the king in his throne room. It must have been very scary for her to take the risk, in light of the fact that the king had not found pleasure in her company for a month. Three days of fasting, and likely prayer are analogous with Jesus' Garden of Gethsemane. It was her Approach to the inmost cave. Going before the king was tantamount to going to her own burial cave, standing in front of it and saying to death, "I am yours; do what you will." Esther knew that Haman unwittingly expected her to die, since she was a Hebrew, pointing, to the fact that Satan expected Christ to die. Christopher Vogler in <u>The Writer's Journey</u> says, "Heroes must die so that they can be reborn." Esther accepts her potential death in order to be reborn as the heroine of her people.

In literary form, *the ordeal* is the climax and center point of Act II of the story. It is the central crisis of the story. We must not confuse this with the climax of the story, which does not happen until Act III. Yet, it is the point at which our protagonist, or heroine, has a transformation of character. It is the event that changes her forever. Our heroine will never be the same person she was in her *ordinary world*. She becomes a new creation. It is symbolic of what I call the macro–Hero's Journey that all Christians share. Our *ordeal* is when we surrender our lives to Christ. We die to our flesh and we are never the same. We are reborn in Christ for a much greater purpose. Romans 8:13 says, "For if you live according to the flesh, you will die, but if by the Spirit you put to death the deeds of the body, you will live." Esther chapter five points us to that marvelous truth.

Esther and the Gospel

The phrase referencing the third day instantly reminds us of the three days Jesus spent in the tomb. Jesus bore God's wrath for three days when he descended into hell. Jesus denied the desires of his flesh, which would be to avoid suffering and death. Instead, he paid the price of our sins and imputed his righteousness to us. God clothed us in Christ; He made us acceptable in the beloved. Esther denied her flesh by fasting for three days, pointing to Jesus denying his flesh. Esther denied herself and put her very life at risk for the sake of her people. Her denial of the flesh points us to Jesus.

If you recall the symbolism of the king's chamber from our last lesson, we saw a picture of the Holy of Holies, that no one could enter unless God made them acceptable. God must deem us acceptable to enter his presence. Esther puts on her royal robes to go before her king, royal robes with which the king clothed her, which signified her acceptance as his chosen queen. This is a picture of God clothing us in righteousness, in the clothing that he provided. The clothing that God provided for us is Jesus himself. We are clothed in Jesus, which makes us able to come into God's presence.

8

Esther 6

Context

Chapter six of Esther satisfies a hunger that has been growing in the past few chapters. We get a resolution to a conflict that has been intensifying. There are four main characters in this chapter: Ahasuerus, Haman, Mordecai, and God. Yes, God. Although the narrative doesn't explicitly mention God, through a plot twist and irony he becomes the central character.

Observations

The first scene opens with the king unable to sleep. He asks his attendants to bring the book of memorable deeds, the chronicles, so they can read them to him. The king may have wanted the reading of the chronicles to lull him to sleep, but in the first twist of irony, it gave him a call to action.

An attendant of the king read the story of when Mordecai discovered a plot by Bigthana and Teresh to lay hands on the king. He reported the plot to the king and thwarted their plans. The king inquired if anyone did anything to reward Mordecai for the good deed, and the king's young men told him that nothing was done for Mordecai. The king developed an urgent desire to reward Mordecai.

Ahasuerus wanted a trusted nobleman to carry out his desire to give honor to one who so faithfully defended the king's life. A deed such as this could not be trusted to just anyone.

The king's young men reported that Haman was standing in the court. The text does not tell us what time it was or how long it was from the time that the king could not sleep until the time that he summoned someone to carry out his bidding, but the impression I get is that it must have been very early in the morning still, maybe before daylight. Haman arrived in the king's court early that morning because he was eager to hang Mordecai. I can picture him pacing the halls of the court, licking his lips over the imminent taste of sweet revenge. When the king called him in, he must have been overflowing with excitement.

Before Haman could ask his favor of the king, Ahasuerus asked him what he should do for a person who the king delights to honor? Haman, in his pride, assumed the king would not want to honor anyone more than himself. Hence, he relays to the king the highest honor he could imagine, one he wanted for himself. He describes an honor that a king would give a first-born son, a prince, who was returning from a major victory at war over an enemy. This is the honor that Haman wanted. He wanted to be honored as a prince, the second highest position in the kingdom, and maybe even heir to the throne.

Haman tells the king to put his own royal robes on the one he delights to honor, just as a king might do for a son. Haman tells the king to put him on his own horse, showing that he is a victor in body and spirit. He asks the king to treat this man no differently than the king himself would be treated if he were returning victorious from war. The honors that Haman described to the king pleased the king, and the king commanded Haman to give these honors to Mordecai, the Jew.

Literary Devices
Irony

Haman's jaw must have hit the floor. This is not what he was expecting. Oh, the irony! Irony is a literary device that can serve several functions in a story, and indeed it does in this case. Dramatic irony in a story is when the reader knows something and the characters don't. We know from the start of this scene that the king wants to honor Mordecai, but Haman does not know this. He assumes the king wants to honor him. As the reader, we see the tension building as we wait for the truth bomb to drop on Haman. Such plot twists add drama, tension, and excitement to a story, and as readers, we feel an immense amount of pleasure as we wait for the other shoe to drop.

Dr. Katherine L. Turner characterizes situational irony as "a long con—a ruse taking place over time. Participants and onlookers do not recognize the irony because its revelation comes at a later moment in time, the unexpected 'twist.' In situational irony, the anticipated outcome contrasts with the end result" In this case, it was the opposite of what Haman expected. Although Esther does not vanquish him yet, we get a sweet taste of victory on behalf of our protagonist. To make a football analogy, it is like our defense got a pick-six off of the opponent's star quarterback.

Irony is a powerful plot device that an author uses to bring far greater significance to events than otherwise would be there. Here, we see the great significance of this scene is God's providence in the lives of our characters. The author never mentions God, but the use of Irony here puts an exclamation point on the notion that God is orchestrating all these events for the good of his people and for his own glory. In God's providence, the king did not reward Mordecai at the time he exposed the plot. And now, God ordains the king could not sleep and hence the attendants read him the story, reminding him to reward Mordecai. God is a palpable character in this scene.

Moreover, the king specifically states in his instructions to Haman to give the honor to Mordecai the Jew. It is further irony that although the king has signed a death decree for all Jews, he wants to reward this Jew for a deed well done.

Theme

The theme is one of exaltation and grace. Ahasuerus wants to honor and exalt Mordecai. He thoughtfully reflects on what to do and asks Haman what he thinks would be exalting. And he gives the exaltation to Mordecai. Sure, Mordecai did a good deed, but to put him on the king's horse and give him the king's robes were rewards of the highest honor. It was an act of grace. It reminds me of when King David asked if there was anyone left from King Saul's family that he could honor. He found Mephibosheth, a nephew who was lame in both feet. David sent for him and gave him a place at his dining table for the rest of his life. Mephibosheth did nothing to deserve such an honor, which is a picture of us and our salvation. We did nothing to deserve it, but we get it as a free gift from God.

Mood

The mood of this scene is one of joy, the joy of justice. We love it when a good guy does a good deed, and we love it even more when an authority recognizes and rewards someone for the deed. We see that the king wants to give a great honor on Mordecai. He has enough stature that he sits at the king's gate, but he is not one who comes and goes from the halls of the king's home quarters. This honor was huge! We can rejoice with Mordecai.

Story Structure and Archetypes

In this chapter, we see a continuation of stage 6 of The Hero's Journey, *tests, allies, and enemies.* This is a stage of The Hero's Journey that can repeat and/or continue until the climax. It is a stage where the author, in this case, God, can add drama and build tension. Ahasuerus, who is a Shapeshifter, emerges as an ally. Until now, his shapeshifting proved to be unsettling or downright disastrous for our heroine. Mordecai continues to be an ally to Esther, and Haman continues to be a shadow character archetype. His wife, sons and friends emerge as shadow characters as well.

Foreboding

The next scene of this chapter, a brief one, provides another literary device, foreboding. Haman's wife and friends tell him. "If Mordecai, before whom you have begun to fall, is of the Jewish people, you will not overcome him but will surely fall before him." This signals that things are not working out so well for Haman and his bitterness towards this Jew. This Benjamite will prove to be Haman the Agagite's undoing.

We learned in chapter two that Mordecai is a Benjamite, a son of Kish. Kish was King Saul's father's name, and the implication is that Mordecai may be a direct descendent of King Saul, the one who conquered and killed all the Amalekites except for King Agag. We can reasonably infer that the hatred Haman had for Mordecai was driven by bitterness towards Jews. We do not know from the text that Haman knew he was a Benjamite. Maybe he knew, and it fueled his bitterness. Yet, we as readers, have this information for a reason. God, in his providence, plans to finish what King Saul neglected to do. God is going to deal with this Agagite and we can see it coming in the aforementioned foreboding statement from Haman's wife.

The last scene of this chapter is the arrival of the king's eunuchs to bring Haman to the feast that Esther prepared. This scene puts an exclamation point on the foreboding from the previous scene. The tide has turned and the tension mounts. God is about to do something great, and we can't wait to see what it is!

Esther and the Gospel

In these scenes, the office of the king reflects a type of God, our Heavenly Father. Haman portrays a type of Satan and Mordecai reflects a type of the Church, Christians collectively and individually. What we see in these three characters is a picture of God exalting and glorifying his Church for faithful loyalty. Of course, it is Christ's faithful loyalty that God imputed to the Church. Satan wants to destroy the Church and get glory for himself. And the Church, represented by Mordecai, receives the robes of the king and the horse of the king while he receives exaltation above the nations. It is a picture of our future glory as believers. It is a picture of the God clothing the Church in Christ's righteousness.

Haman had to lead Mordecai through the city by the reigns of the king's horse, showing homage and glory to the rider. This is a bit of foreshadowing of the assertion that we find in Philippians 2:10 & 11, "So that at the name of Jesus every knee should bow, in heaven and on earth and under the earth, and every tongue confess that Jesus Christ is Lord, to the glory of God the Father."

9

Esther 7

Context

In the previous chapter (6), we did not see an appearance of our Heroine. Yes, at this point we can call her a heroine because she approached the inmost cave and went through her ordeal. She faced death and stood in the breach for her people. Esther put her own needs aside for her people and that's what heroes do. Whether her actions are successful is secondary. We will find out later if she succeeds, but for now, we see a heroine who has put it all on the line for God's covenant family.

The first five verses of chapter seven illustrate to us that Esther is wise and cunning, and I do not mean cunning is a negative way. She fasted and likely prayed about her meeting with her husband and king, and has likely gotten advice from her mentor, Mordecai. She went into the feast with a plan, and she executed it flawlessly.

Esther prepared a feast for Ahasuerus and Haman two consecutive days, building up and honoring her king. She gave him the respect he was due, a principal that God gives us in Ephesians 5:33. "...and let the wife see that she *respects* her husband." The respect she gave her husband came back to her multiplied in terms of favor and love.

Observations

Esther did not speak of what she wanted for two days, and after they had been drinking wine on the second day, her king finally asked what he could do for her. Again, he offered anything up to half of his kingdom. The time was right, and she set the scene to give him an answer. Ahasuerus had been drinking wine, and she knew that in times like this he was prone to making emotional decisions, extreme decisions. She had his favor, rightly earned, and it was time to make her request.

Esther asked the king to spare her life. In all humility, she said that she would be content being a slave under her king but wanted him to spare her life. Ahasuerus did not know what she was talking about, not knowing she was Jewish. He asked her who had sold her life, and she dropped the truth bomb, "This wicked Haman!"

Don't you wish you could have been there to see the look on his face? At least we get the next best thing. The author tells us that Haman was terrified. Such a descriptive word, terrified. It is a familiar and memorable feeling for us all. We know what it looks like on the face of others. Haman had to be shaking in his sandals. But what next? How will the king react?

Ahasuerus must have wanted to rip Haman's throat out. "And the king arose in his wrath from the wine-drinking and went into the palace garden..." We get a second mention of wine-drinking on purpose. Most of us have had the unpleasant experience of seeing how alcohol can inflame a man's anger. The author paints that picture for us here. We can imagine the king storming out of the door, pacing back and forth, clinching his fists in rage and cursing the day Haman was born.

It would not have taken too long for him to realize that Haman had tricked him into condemning the Jews to death, including his own wife, and that his irrevocable order is coming back to haunt him. He now realizes that his beautiful wife is a Jew. Wrath gave way to rage, and rage gave way to wanting retribution. He returned to the place where they were drinking wine with a purpose in his heart to deal with Haman. What he found would add fuel to the fire that burned is his heart.

The text tells us that Haman was falling on Esther on the couch when we came into the room. The text does not tell us what Haman was doing exactly. It could have been that he was assaulting her, intending to hurt her. Or he could have been throwing himself at her mercy, literally and figuratively. Another possibility is that he may have even been sexually assaulting her out of anger. Exactly what he was doing was not pertinent. The king saw what he thought was an attack, and his sentence of justice was swift and sure. He gave orders to hang Haman.

If you have ever watched a few episodes of Downton Abby, you understand what could be a universal truth, that the servants in the home of a wealthy family know more about what is going on than the family itself. We find this is true in the king's palace. Harbona, one of the king's eunuchs, reveals to Ahasueras a fact that the king may not have known before. Harbona told the king that Haman had built a gallows at his house where he intended to hang Mordecai. Perfect! Just as Haman's plan to bring honor to himself instead went to Mordecai, his plan to hang Mordecai on the 50-cubit gallows came back to haunt him or *hang him*.

Literary Elements
Theme

The theme of this scene is celebratory. Esther, the king, and Haman are in the palace enjoying an extravagant feast and wine drinking that lasts for a couple of days. The king tells Esther that she can have anything she wants up to half the kingdom. This reminds us that as the bride of Christ, we have an inheritance. We are joint heirs to the kingdom. This scene points to the marriage supper of the lamb where we come into our inheritance. This scene points to when God separates the sheep from the goats.

Mood

The mood of this scene is anticipation. We know what Esther is up to. We know about the foreshadowing from the previous chapter. Esther set the stage and the three key characters are present. We see a masterful arranging of events by our heroine as she closes in on her goal. We are building to the ultimate climax of the story, although we will reach the full climax later. This chapter brings us to a preliminary, anticipatory climax.

Poetic Justice

Poetic justice is a literary device that sets up the punishment of evil deeds and a rewarding of righteous deeds. That is exactly what we get here, poetic justice. It is not a singular act of justice in which God punishes an evil act, but it is a double exchange involving justice and reward. Using this literary device not only magnifies the beauty and impact of Haman's justice, but it also points to the double exchange that Christ accomplishes for us. He takes the penalty of our sin, and in exchange, he imputes his righteousness to us, a double transaction. Readers of Esther feel overjoyed with the poetic justice in chapter seven. It is joy sublime!

Story Structure

Esther does not enter a new stage of The Hero's Journey in this chapter. Rather, we see the plot continue to develop through *tests, allies, and enemies*. The tension is rising as we move towards the next stage, *the reward, seizing the sword*.

Character Archetypes

Esther continues to portray the heroine archetype; Ahasuerus continues as a shapeshifter and Haman as a shadow character. Harbona becomes an ally to Esther when he informs the king of Haman's gallows and his intentions. Regarding the servants of the house, they know more about what is going on than the masters of the house. Here, it is easy to imagine that the servants close to Esther knew everything, and they were on her side. After all, they had carried messages back and forth from Mordecai. They were her allies.

Esther and the Gospel

This scene illustrates how a godly bride behaves. Remember when we talked about chapter one having an illustration of a husband and wife behaving badly? It was an illustration of how Adam and Eve behaved in the garden. He did not protect her, and she did not respect him. This was true for Ahasuerus and Vashti, just as it was for Adam and Eve.

In chapter seven of Esther, we see the king and Esther portray a picture of a redeemed bride and groom The king protects his bride and his bride respects him. His reward is a perfect and beautiful bride. Her reward is that he made her a joint heir in the kingdom. Romans 8: 16 & 17 says, "The Spirit himself bears witness with our spirit that we are children of God, and if children - heirs of God and fellow heirs with Christ, provided we suffer him in order that we also may be glorified with him." This scene points to this wonderful truth.

10

Esther 8

Context

Chapter eight opens with the king giving Haman's house to Esther and giving the signet ring to Mordecai. Esther tells the king Mordecai is her uncle, and she puts him over the house that once was Haman's. Esther throws herself at the mercy of the king and begs him to rescind the decree of the destruction of the Jews. Ahasuerus cannot rescind his decree, but he offers for Mordecai to write a new law, whatever law he wants to write to give the Jews a defense.

Mordecai summons the scribes, and he writes a law in the king's name that allows the Jews to use lethal force to defend themselves on the thirteenth day of the twelfth month. They sent the new law out to all provinces and in all languages, and the Jews is Susa rejoiced.

Observations

We know that going before the king could lead to death if he does not raise the royal scepter as his declaration of approval and granting life. This reminds us of Esther putting her life on the line, as a type of Christ, on behalf of her people. When he raised the scepter, he invited her to make her request known in more detail.

Esther asks the king to revoke his orders to destroy the Jewish people on the appointed day. The king is in a conundrum. He desires to grant Esther and her people a reprieve, but he has already issued a law, and a Persian king cannot revoke even his own law. This reminds us that God has an immutable law that he must punish sin by death, and God cannot revoke his own law. Just as God would have to make another way to save his covenant children, the king must find another way to save the Jews. The king found another way, illustrating how God found another way.

God, in his providence, shows his handiwork again by being an invisible central character in the story. Mordecai writes a new law and presents it to Ahasueras, a law that I don't think anyone would be bold enough to present to the king unless God directed it.

The new law gives the Jewish people the right to defend their lives from anyone who would seek to do them harm. Mordecai's law gives them the right to kill whoever attacks them and the right to plunder all of their goods. Ahasuerus agrees to the law and they seal it with the king's signet ring, pointing us to the truth we read in Romans 8:2, "For the law of the spirit of life has set you free in Christ Jesus from the law of sin and death."

Literary Elements
Theme

A theme of legal action permeates chapter eight. The author reminds us that the king cannot reverse even his own law and he announces he will allow a new law. The new law is for all the people in all 127 provinces. He has messengers send copies of the law out in all languages. It is all very official.

Mood

The mood swings back to celebration. The Jews celebrate in Susa and in every province. They rejoiced at the edict, and they had feasts and a holiday. There was so much celebration that even those who were not Jewish, claimed to be Jews. The king gave Mordecai robes of fine linen, white, blue, and purple, and he rides through the city to celebrate.

Story Structure

Chapter eight brings us to the 9th stage of The Hero's Journey, *the reward*. This stage is sometimes also called *seizing the sword*. This stage is where heroes earn the reward for their willingness to lay down their lives for the cause. It is the moment that heroes take possession of what it was they were seeking when they crossed over to the new world. For our heroine, she saves her people from destruction.

When I introduced The Hero's Journey story structure, I mentioned the stages might not come in order, sometimes skipped, or even repeated. In Esther's story, God compresses the final four stages. Stage 10 is *the road back* and Stage 11 is the *resurrection*. *The road back* is the hero's journey back to the ordinary world as a changed person, although sometimes a hero stays in the new world.

Ester remains in her new world as a queen. Yet she has a metaphorical return to the ordinary world in that she reveals to the king that she is a Jew and returns to her true identity.

One aspect of *the road back* stage is that the hero returns to the ordinary world with the news of the reward. The king fulfils this aspect of th*e road back* by sending the news to all 127 provinces in their own languages. This is a depiction of Esther returning to her people with the good news, which is *seizing the sword* in the Hero's Journey structure.

Esther and the Gospel

In the closing scene of this chapter, the king dresses Mordecai in fine linen robes of white and blue and purple. Mordecai here is a picture of the Church, the Bride of Christ. Revelation 19:7 & 8 says, "" Let us rejoice and exult and give him the glory. For the marriage supper of the Lamb has come. And his bride he has made ready; it was granted to her to clothe herself with fine linen, bright and pure "–for the fine linen is the righteous deeds of the saints."

The letters written to all 127 provinces are also a picture of when Jesus told his disciples to go forth with the good news in Acts 1:8, "...and you will be my witnesses in Jerusalem and in all Judea and in Samaria, and to the ends of the earth." News of salvation to God's covenant children in Esther's day pointed to when the gospel good news through Jesus comes to us all. Esther's story points us to the fulfillment of God's redemptive plan in Christ Jesus.

We see here a picture of the Old and New Covenants. The Old Covenant was based on the law that God gave to Moses. But it was impossible for God's children to keep the law; therefore, it condemned them to death, except for grace through faith. The New Covenant is a covenant of grace through faith brought to us through the blood of Jesus. The same grace and faith save God's covenant children in both Old and New Covenants.

By enacting the new law, the king agrees to sacrifice his own people, possibly even his own children, to allow the Hebrews to save themselves. He agrees the Jews can take the lives of his people and to plunder from them. He allows them to plunder the wealth of his kingdom. In short, he agrees to a law that is going to be very costly to himself. This is a picture of God finding a very costly solution that saves his covenant people through the sacrifice of his own son, Jesus.

11
Esther 9:1-19

Context

As I have said before, the story in the book of Esther is a story that depicts how God deals with his covenant children. It has elements of the whole Bible compressed into ten chapters. Chapter nine doubles down by referencing many aspects of God's redemptive story, showcasing his glory, majesty, grace, and mercy.

Chapter nine brings us to the date in which the king's first decree and his second decree go into effect. On the thirteenth day of the month of Adar, the Persians attacked the Jews. The new edit allowed the Jews to defend themselves with lethal force and God gave Israel a decisive victory.

Observations

Verse one of chapter nine begins with a reference to the twelfth month. The rest of the chapter has other references to symbolic numbers. The number twelve in the Bible symbolizes perfection, power, and authority. Twelve brings to mind the Twelve Tribes of Israel, the twelve apostles, the twelve stones of remembrance in Joshua, and other instances. I believe the reference to the twelfth month means that God's timing was perfect, and in his power, he delivered Israel. There are parallels to the story of Joshua crossing the Jordan into the promised land and striking fear in the Amorites. When Israel crossed over the Jordan with the Ark of the Covenant, God caused the Jordan to stop flowing so they could cross over on dry land. After the crossing, Joshua called on a representative of each of the twelve tribes to find a stone, and he directed them to stack them up in the riverbed where they carried the Ark across.

Joshua 4:21-24 says, "And he said to the people of Israel, "When your children ask their fathers in times to come, 'what do these stones mean? Then you shall let your children know Israel passed over the Jordan on dry ground.' For the Lord your God dried up the waters of the Jordan for you until you passed over, as the Lord your God did the Red Sea, which he dried up until we passed over, so that all the peoples of the earth may know that the hand of the Lord is mighty, that you may fear the Lord your God forever."

Joshua said they called the place Gilgal. In Joshua chapter five, we read that the kings of the Amorites fell into great fear of Israel upon hearing about God giving them a safe crossing on dry ground. Esther nine verse two says, "...for fear of them had fallen on all peoples." These events reflect what happened in Joshua's day. Both stories show us that God's timing is perfect, his power to save is perfect and his kingship is one of divine authority. And we see fear fall on the enemies of God's children.

The text takes a brief detour from the high-level summary of the victory, including the killing of 500 in the capital of Susa, to give the details of the killing of the ten sons of Haman, calling them all by name. Haman represents a type of Satan in Esther's story. Hence, we can deduce that his ten sons represent those directly under his leadership who *would* carry out the destruction of God's chosen people. Esther, who is a type of Christ, intervenes for her people and her actions result in the destruction of Israel's enemies. She gives us a picture of God's redemptive plan to destroy our enemy, Satan.

The number ten (sons) points us to the beast in Revelation that has seven heads and ten horns. Revelation 17: 12-14 says, "And the ten horns that you see are the ten kings who have not yet received royal power, but they are to receive authority as kings for one hour, together with the beast. These are of one mind and hand over their power and authority to the beast. They will make war on the Lamb, and the Lamb will conquer them, for he is the Lord of lords and King of kings, and those with him are called chosen and faithful."

Esther conquers the ten sons of Haman, and Haman was a type of Satan. This represents when Christ conquers Satan, the beast and the ten kings who are of one mind with the beast.

The first half of Esther 9 is a reference to the disobedience of humankind that Christ redeems. One of the many lovely truths of God's redemptive story of his people is that the disobedience of his children in the first Adam finds redemption in the obedience imputed to his children by the second Adam, Christ.

Mordecai and Esther are Benjamites, and they likely descended from Saul. Haman was an Amalekite and a descendent of Agag. If you recall, King Saul, a Benjamite and king of Israel, received instructions from God to attack and kill the Amalekites led by king Agag. God told him to destroy all the people and all the spoils, but he disobeyed. He let Agag live and Israel took the spoils.

When the Jews defended themselves from their enemies in Persia, they killed many thousands, but they did not take any spoil, even though King Ahasuerus had decreed that they could. They redeemed the previous unfaithfulness of Saul.

Literary Elements
Theme

Chapter nine of Esther continues with a theme of numbers that points us to specific aspects of God's redemptive history. We see the numbers twelve, thirteen, and ten. We already explored the meaning of the numbers, twelve and ten. I previously commented, tongue-in-cheek, that thirteen was Israel's unlucky number. Of course, with a providential God, there is no such thing as luck. The number thirteen in the Bible, depending on the commentator you read, can represent

Satan, evil, rebellion, or lawlessness. In Ester, it represents the evil date of Israel's destruction, and it points us to the evil one who is behind it.

Mood and Poetic Justice

Poetic justice is the mood of the first nineteen verses. Just as we saw with Haman, he was ready to kill the Jews on the day he had decreed for their destruction, but it turned into the day of their triumphant victory. As we saw before, God uses the literary tool of poetic justice to amplify our feeling of joy in response to victory over evil.

Story Structure

The first nineteen verses of chapter nine take us into the eleventh stage of The Hero's Journey, *resurrection*. This stage is the climax of the story that comes in the third act. It is the stage in which the heroine achieves a second victory over death, a resurrection from an actual or metaphorical death. For Esther, we see her and the Jews defeat the death sentence for all of God's covenant children.

Esther has now almost completed her transformation, or what in literary study we call the character arch. She began her journey in her ordinary world as a simple Hebrew girl living in exile in Persia. The call to adventure takes Esther into a new world where she grows, changes, and becomes a heroine. She returns to the old world with the elixir that saves her world.

In Esther's case, she integrates the old and the new worlds. She remains queen and yet she begins to live according to her ethnic heritage. She metaphorically returns to her old world by returning to her roots, her identity as a Jew, yet she remains in the new world as queen. Her journey is nearly complete.

Esther and the Gospel

In the Old Testament, God lays out the roles and functions of three offices: prophet, priest, and king. In simple terms, the function of the prophet is to speak forth for God, calling us to repentance and faith. The function of the priest is to intercede for God's chosen people and atone for their sins through the sacrificial law. The role of the king is to lead and protect his kingdom and to conquer their enemies.

God gave us many examples of what it looks like to perform these roles. There are books in the Old Testament named for major and minor prophets, and there are many more prophets that do not have books written by them. The prophets speak to us for God, relaying what he has told them to say. Often, the message is that his chosen people should repent from their sins and have faith in God.

We have many examples of priests, such as Aaron, Eleazar and Abiathar. Their function was to offer sacrifices for the remission of sins. They stood in the gap between a most holy God and sinful people who could not come into his presence.

We have many examples of kings, both good and bad. King David is the most notable king we see in the Old Testament. He gives us a robust picture of what kings do. He ruled over his kingdom, took care of his subjects and he conquered their enemies, the Philistines, by making war with them.

It was always God's plan to merge these three offices in his Son, Jesus. Every prophet, priest, and king of old point us to what Jesus did for us on the cross and through His resurrection. God spoke to us through him; in fact, he is the living Word of God. Jesus intercedes for us and makes atonement for our sins. He is our king who will wage victorious war on our enemies. We see these offices represented in Christ upon his return as described in Revelation 19: 11-16.

"Then I saw heaven opened, and behold, a white horse! The one sitting on it is called Faithful and True, and in righteousness he judges and makes war. His eyes are like a flame of fire, and on his head are many diadems, and he has a name written that no one knows but himself. He is clothed in a robe dipped in blood, and the name by which he is called is The Word of God. And the armies of heaven, arrayed in fine linen, white and pure, were following him on white horses. From his mouth comes a sharp sword with which to strike down the nations, and he will rule them with a rod of iron. He will tread the winepress of the fury of the wrath of God the Almighty. On his robe and on his thigh, he has a name written, King of kings and Lord of lords."

In Esther nine, we see Esther portray a picture of these three offices, pointing us to Jesus. She acts as a prophetess by speaking to Mordecai and her people, telling them to fast and presumably pray. As a priest, she intercedes for God's people with King Ahasuerus to save them from a death sentence. Symbolizing a king, she secures the destruction of the enemies of God's people, pointing us to the kingly role of Jesus. She provides a marvelous picture of God's providential, redemptive plan, making God the primary character in a story in which the author never mentions him by name. Just as what we call, *general revelation* in God's creation declares his glory and existence, Esther reveals his providence and proclaims his glory.

12

Esther 9: 20-32 & Chapter 10

Context

The second half of chapter nine and the brief chapter ten tell the story of how Mordecai sent letters and commanded the Jews to keep the fourteenth and fifteenth days of Adar as a celebration, in which they would give gifts of food and gifts to the poor. This passage recounts the reason for the celebration of Purim. The author is wrapping up and putting a bow on the story, with details of the official documentation.

Observations

Purim is the name they gave to the celebration of the casting of pur. Haman, the enemy of the Jews, cast pur, or lots, to determine when he would destroy the Jews. Yet in the perfect twist of irony, casting pur sealed his own destruction. God's sovereignty over creation is magnified through the use of irony.

It is sublimely ironic that Haman cast lots to find the most providential time to kill the Jews, but God, in his providence, uses the casting of lots to establish the time that he would conquer their enemy. This points us to the occasion of Satan conspiring to use Christ's crucifixion to thwart God's plan to redeem his people, but God redeems his people through Satan's plot. Casting lots seems to be an act of random chance, yet there is no random chance in God's plans. He planned for everything. The celebration of Purim is a celebration of providence.

Literary Elements
Theme

The second half of chapter nine reveals the theme of official business, of documentation and recording. Mordecai sent letters to all provinces, adjuring all the Jews to celebrate the two days that followed the routing of their enemies. Esther followed suit and sent letters to all 127 provinces instructing the Jews to celebrate what they called Purim.

Mood

The mood of this passage is one of gladness and rejoicing. The Jews went from being victims to victors overnight. This change for the Jews points to the same change from mourning to gladness as depicted throughout scripture. Jeremiah 31:13 says, "Then shall the young women rejoice in the dance, and the young men and the old shall be merry. I will turn their mourning into joy; I will comfort them and give them gladness for sorrow." This is the mood the entire counsel of scripture means to impart to us. John 16:20 affirms, "Truly, truly, I say to you, that you will weep and lament, but the world will rejoice; you will grieve, but your grief will be turned into joy."

Story Structure

The final stage of The Hero's Journey, *return with the elixir* happens in chapter 9. This is the point at which a hero returns to his ordinary world with the elixir that saves the ordinary world. Our heroine returns with the elixir, news of the salvific plan to save her people. She and Mordecai sent out letters with evidence that they were saved, and they should celebrate it! Purim actually points to God's providence. Hence, the elixir that Esther returns to her ordinary world with is a perpetual celebration of God's providential plan to save his people.

Our heroine's journey is complete. Esther has traveled from her ordinary world to a new world and back again, encountering shadow characters, shapeshifters, allies, and enemies. She braved the journey into the inmost cave and she embraced her ordeal. Esther died to self and lived for her people. Her symbolic resurrection brought resurrection to all of her kindred living in Persia. Our heroine gives us inspiration and an example to follow.

Esther and the Gospel

Esther's Hero's Journey points us to Jesus' Hero's Journey. It points us to God's plan of redemption accomplished through the death and resurrection of his son Jesus. In fact, all of the Hero's in the Old Testament point to Jesus. Abraham, Jacob, Joseph, Moses, Joshua, and King David all had Hero's Journeys that point us to Jesus.

We too have Hero's Journeys which began when we crossed the threshold into a new world, when we answered that irresistible call to accept Christ as savior. As heroes, we all faced our approaches to the inmost cave and received the call to seize the sword. And God calls us to return to our ordinary world with the elixir that saves, the same elixir that Christ returned with, his Saving Blood. We are to share it with our family, friends, community, and world.

Chapter ten displays a few footnotes to the entire story. One of them is a profound message of hope for us as Christians. The text tells us that Mordecai was second in rank to the king, and that he was great and popular among the Jews., He represents the bride of Christ, the Church. We see Mordecai foretelling the glory we will have in Christ.

II Timothy 2:11, 12 says, "The saying is trustworthy for: If we have died with him, we will also live with him; if we endure, we will also reign with him..." This passage in II Timothy tells us we will reign with Christ, second in command to God. The picture of Mordecai points us to this truth.

We have this truth affirmed for us in the Heidelberg Catechism, question 32: "But why are you called a Christian? A. Because by faith I am a member of Christ and so I share in his anointing. I am anointed to confess his name, to present myself to him as a living sacrifice of thanks, to strive with a good conscience against sin and the devil.

in this life, and afterward to reign with Christ over all creation for all eternity."

The book of Esther ends by pointing us to this most wonderful hope.

About the Author

Jim Dent is a native of Rome, GA where he lives with his wife of 32 years, Ali. He received his bachelor's degree from The University of Georgia and master's degree from Kennesaw State College. He is a deacon at First Presbyterian Church and formerly served as a missionary with Mercy Ships.

www.ingramcontent.com/pod-product-compliance
Lightning Source LLC
Chambersburg PA
CBHW050556160726
48003CB00002B/922